Becoming Human

AN INVITATION TO CHRISTIAN ETHICS

William E. May

Pflaum Publishing,
Dayton, Ohio

Pflaum Publishing, Dayton, Ohio 45439

Library of Congress Catalog
Card Number: 74-82489

ISBN: 0-8278-0002-9

Design: Tim Potter
Printed in the United States of America.

To my wife, Patricia

TABLE OF CONTENT

Introduction|VI

1. Christ and Our Moral Being|1

2. Knowing the Human|25

3. Growing Into the Human Conscientiously|53

4. Becoming Human In and Through Our Deeds|79

5. Becoming Human In a Real World|113

   Bibliography |143

INTRODUCTION

Some words, observes Herbert McCabe in his beautiful *What Is Ethics All About?*, are "growing" words. That is, they point to realities of such richness, such depth, that they are almost inexhaustible in their intelligibility and meaning. Among these is the word "human." What does it mean to be a human being? No one, of course, can give a definitive, final answer to this question. But the inability to do so does not mean that the word is vague or indefinite in meaning. We can certainly say what it does *not* mean, and we know in part what it does mean. We are continually growing in our understanding and appreciation of its meaning.

Growth in understanding what it means to be a human being is part of our own personal search for identity. Each of us is engaged in that search, and in it we are helped by our fellowmen. The search of the individual human being for his own identity is both personal and communal, or corporate, for our existence is a co-existence, our being is a being with. In discovering ourselves, we also discover the identity of the entire human race.

For the Christian the incarnation of the Father's Word illumines not only the meaning of God but also the meaning of man. Growth in humanhood is viewed by the Christian as growth toward the destiny that man has because he is the created image of a loving God; each man has a vocation, a call, and it is by answering this call that he becomes fully human.

In this work I have tried to present Christian ethics as an invitation to become human, to answer the call rooted in us by virtue of our very being. In the initial chapter, an attempt is made to show how Christian ethics is related to what we can call the general moral strivings of mankind, that is, the efforts of living human beings everywhere to find meaning in their lives, to discover their identity. Here the significance of the incarnation as an event bringing light to the meaning of human existence is examined. In the second chapter, reflections on the way in which we come to know the human are offered. The purpose of this chapter is to show that value judgments and moral evaluations of concrete situations are not capricious or arbitrary opinions dependent on purely relativistic considerations but are rooted in the truth, in what we can call reality-making or truth-making factors. In this chapter, an effort is made to show that the empirical research of contemporary developmental psychologists lends support to the solid philosophical and theological positions developed by writers in the natural law tradition.

The third chapter is concerned with the important role that conscience has to play in our moral lives. Here again the relevant work of contemporary psychologists and psychoanalysts is shown to support the best in philosophical and theological inquiry. The social or communal dimensions of the development of conscience are emphasized, and reflections are given on the knotty problem of the rights of the individual conscience and the role of authority, in particular of Church authority in moral questions.

The fourth chapter deals with the evaluation of our human acts. From the perspective of normative ethics or of ethical methodology, this is the central chapter in the work. It seeks to show what reality-making or truth-making factors simply must be taken into account in an objective, truthful appraisal of moral situations and offers criticisms of what the author regards as inadequate views. In particular it seeks to counter what the author considers a dangerous consequentialist tendency in a great deal of contemporary writing by Catholic moral theologians.

The final chapter is concerned with the real world in which we become human. Here attention is focused more on the noncognitive dimensions of our existence as moral beings and on the mystery of human freedom, the reality of sin and grace, and the need for support in our struggle to become human. Here, too, the relevance of some behavioristic studies for understanding our moral life is discussed, particularly to find what analogies exist between what behaviorists call "reinforcers" of behavior and what theologians call sin and grace. In this chapter, too, the political-social structure of human existence is taken into account.

A word of gratitude is necessary here: gratitude to my students who have courteously listened to me as I have attempted to articulate the struggle of men to become human; gratitude to writers like Herbert McCabe, Paul Ramsey, Germain Grisez, Charles Curran, and many others who have helped me to understand the issues at stake; gratitude to my wife, Patricia, and to my seven children for their encouragement and support; gratitude, finally, to the God Who is our Emmanuel, for his goodness to me and to all men.

Chapter One:

CHRIST AND OUR MORAL BEING

The significance of Jesus for our moral life or, better, our moral being, can be approached in many different ways. One could, for example, focus attention on the teaching of Jesus, in particular his call for conversion, his insistence that we put first the kingdom or reign of God, his challenge to love.[1] Or one could reflect on the meaning that Jesus has for our moral lives as Lord and redeemer, as sanctifier and justifier, as brother and servant.[2] Finally one could, as I intend to do, seek to explore the significance of Jesus as the light of the world, as the one who illumines human existence. In order to carry out this exploratory venture it will first be necessary to think about what it means to be a human being, for this is what we are and this is what Jesus himself is, unless one regards him as did the docetists—and to be a docetist is the perennial temptation of the Christian—as not *really* a man but simply as a God who temporarily took leave of heaven to walk the earth in the outward form of man and who now, as risen Lord, is "full-time" God again. After this preliminary inquiry we can then try to see what is meant when we say that Jesus is the perfect man and when we confess that this man Jesus is the personal, incarnate Word of the Father whose life he is and whose life he offers us through himself and the Spirit that is his and his Father's gift to us. Some concluding comments about the relationship of Christian ethics to what can be termed the "moral strivings" of mankind can then be offered.

I

To be a human being is to be an animal. But a human being, as René Dubos so beautifully puts it, is so *human* an animal.[3] A human being is an animal, but an animal *with a difference*. This difference can be expressed in different ways, but one major and critically important way of putting this difference is to say that man, and man alone of all animals, is a moral being. That man, and man alone, is a moral being is illustrated in common speech. It is meaningful, for instance, to speak about making human life human. Yet to speak in this way seems paradoxical. We would find it odd, indeed absurd, were someone to speak about making bovine life bovine or canine life canine. A cow, after all, is a cow and a dog is a dog. Yet it is not absurd or meaningless to speak about making human life human. Since it does make sense to speak in this fashion, it follows that man is indeed a unique kind of animal, and it also follows that the word *human* must be used in two quite distinct ways when we talk about making human life human. The second use of the term implies that a human being is not totally "human" when he comes into existence. Certainly no one who uses the term *human* in this second sense wants to deny that all men are equally human beings simply from the fact that they are all identifiably men, i.e., members of the same biological species. Yet he is affirming that "being human" is not something factually given but is rather a process, a growth, a matter of an individual human being "becoming" human. To use the term in this second sense is to imply that there is a process of humanization; it is to imply that a human being has a destiny to which he is called and that he fulfills his being by his struggle to attain this destiny. In addition, to distinguish between two meanings of the term *human* is to affirm that not everything that man does and can do is really human. It is to distinguish between *is* and *ought*, between what men actually are and do, and what men ought to be and ought to do. It is, in short, to assert that man is a moral being, that human existence is a moral existence, that human history is a moral history.

But who is to tell us what being "human" in the second sense of this term is? Surely any one individual or group of individuals would be both foolish and arrogant were he to claim that he and he alone knew precisely what being human in this sense entails. Yet the search for the human in this sense is not meaningless or absurd. Man's strivings to find his identity and to discover meaning in life are not, as Jean-Paul Sartre would have them, "useless passions."[4] Progress or growth in understanding the meaning of the human is possible, and it is possible because man, as the inquiring, questioning being, is the being who has within himself the preconditions making progress possible. To see what I mean here a passage from Bernard Lonergan is helpful, inasmuch as it sheds light on the dynamism that moves the human animal ever onward in his quest for meaning, truth, and responsible action. Lonergan writes:

> Spontaneously we move from experiencing to
> the effort to understand; and this spontaneity

is not unconscious or blind; on the contrary, it is constitutive of our conscious intelligence; just as the absence of the effort to understand is constitutive of stupidity. Spontaneously we move from understanding with its manifold and conflicting expressions to critical reflection; again, the spontaneity is not unconscious or blind; it is constitutive of our critical rationality, of the demand within us for sufficient reason, a demand that operates prior to any formulation of a principle of sufficient reason; and it is the neglect or absence of this demand that constitutes silliness. Spontaneously we move from judgments of fact or possibility to judgments of value and to the deliberateness of decision and commitment; and that spontaneity is not unconscious or blind; it constitutes us as conscientious, responsible persons, and its absence would leave us psychopaths.[5]

My purpose here is not to comment at length on this passage (in another chapter we will look at it again from a somewhat different perspective). Although many questions could be asked about it, its major thrust is clear. Human civilization, culture, progress are possible because man is the being who asks questions, who inquires, who seeks to understand his experience, to test his understanding of experience for its truth, and to act responsibly in accord with a true understanding of himself and his world. And the dynamism that makes this movement from experience to responsible action possible, "far from being the product of cultural advance, is the condition of its possibility."[6]

The questions that man asks of his experience are

4

of various sorts. Some are meaningful and can be given quick, final, definite yes-no answers: Is it raining outside? What is the chemical composition of table salt? Others are meaningful, yet they can be answered only partially; the final, definitive answers can never be given simply because the questions reach out for or intend the unknown whole or totality of which our answers reveal only a part. Questions of this kind, called "transcendental" by Lonergan, move us from what we know to seek what we do not know yet. They are concerned with realities that are so rich in meaning, in intelligibility, that they are seemingly inexhaustible. They employ what Herbert McCabe calls "growing" words, words like "love" or "loyalty" or "justice."[7]

Although these questions will never be given a final answer, this does not mean that they cannot be answered at all in a meaningfully true way. An example will help. I, for instance, am a father, standing in a certain relationship to my children. I do not believe that it is possible to give a definitive answer to the question, What is a father? But I do think that it is possible to tell with truth some things that this cannot mean: It cannot mean battering my children senseless if they disturb my watching an NFL game. Similarly the final answer to the question concerning the meaning of the human cannot be given; still it is true to say, without being accused of being a wooden-headed legalist bent on stifling human creativity and freedom, that it cannot mean barbecuing neonates in order to test the psychological effect this has on their mothers, nor can it mean cheating the poor or stoning an adulteress.

Our inquiring existence, moreover, is not solipsistic. As John Donne put it, "no man is an island." In our constant search for meaning and for truth we are joined by our fellowmen. Indeed, the world in which we live today is not, as Lonergan notes,[8] a world of pure, unmediated experience, but is rather a world that is mediated to us by meaning, the meaning that our fathers and mothers, our grandparents, the whole human race before us, have discovered. We can question this meaning in the light of our own experiences and test it for its truth, but we do not start from scratch.[9]

Man, the inquiring social animal, differs from all other animals even in his corporate existence. For man is not merely gregarious; he is social; he lives in community—or perhaps even more accurately in a network of communities—and his existence is a coexistence, his being is a being with. What ultimately makes his existence differ so markedly from that of other animals is his ability to speak. Man is the linguistic animal. Why is this of such critical significance? Listen to these words of Herbert McCabe, for I think that they express this significance eloquently:

Man is the linguistic animal. When we say this we are not just pointing to a distinguishing characteristic of man. . . . Language does not only distinguish man from other animals, it distinguishes his animality from that of other animals. To be a man is to be an animal in a new sense, to be alive in a new sense. This means that even the activities which a man seems to share with other animals are transfigured by the fact that they are part of an animality that finally issues in language. Man does not just *add* speech on to such things as eating and sexual behavior; the fact that these latter occur in a linguistic context makes a difference to what they are.[10]

McCabe goes on to point out that the "world" of animals is a world that is shaped or constituted in large measure by the animals' perception of it. This is true of man's world also, and like all other animals man seeks to share this world with his fellows through communication—indeed, it is only through communication with his fellows that he comes to "know" this world.[11] But in man this communication reaches a new intensity, inasmuch as it becomes language. And, McCabe remarks,

It is important to see language not first of all in terms of the operation that is peculiar to it—the transfer of messages—but to see it as a mode of communication, a sharing of life. With the appearance of language we come to a . . . radical change, a change in which we do not merely see something new but have a new way of seeing, in which something is produced whch could not be envisaged in the old terms and which changes our whole way of envisaging what has gone before. . . . /it is/a new kind of life.[12]

The point that McCabe is trying to put across may be clearer if we distinguish human language from the kind of communication or transferal of messages operative, for example, in computer data-bank retrieval systems. In these systems there is certainly communication in the sense that messages are delivered or transferred from one entity to another, that information is given and received, and that "knowledge" in a sense is accumulated. But the communication involved here is far different from the communication that takes place through human speech and language (and, it ought to be noted, men speak to one another not only through words but through their actions). Human language is not simply a matter of communicating a message; it is above all a matter of communicating the *messenger*. Human language issues beyond communication in *communion*.

Communion among human beings is the ultimate purpose of human speech. This communion is achieved through understanding and love. Human beings are indeed interested in *what* is being said, but our basic interest reaches beyond the what to the *who* is saying it. Through our speech we reveal ourselves both to ourselves and to others, and vice versa. Through language we discover who we are and who we are meant to be. Our being as the human animal, the moral being, is a linguistic being. To be a man, to be the animal who is a moral being, is to be a being who can communicate and share life.

II

At this point we are in a position to think about the meaning that Jesus has for our moral lives, for our being as the uniquely moral and linguistic animal. Jesus is, like us, a man. But for us Christians he is the "perfect" man. At one time in the history of the Christian Church Jesus' perfection as man was thought to consist in the most perfect kind of knowledge, of power, of strength. Yet to say that Jesus, for example, held the Copernican view of the universe or affirmed the Einsteinian theory of relativity seems absurd. Like us, he too had to "grow" into the human. The meaning of his perfection as man, consequently, must consist in something other than the possession of the most perfect kind of knowledge or beauty or strength. Perhaps the answer lies in his perfection as a "linguistic" being, as a person who expressed most perfectly the meaning of man as the being who is summoned to communicate and share life. In trying to think our way through on this matter we will be helped, I believe, by reflecting on some comments that McCabe has to offer. He first of all distinguishes between the making of a perfect doorknob and the making of a perfect man. It is not as though God, after making a long series of defective men, finally came across the right recipe and made the perfect man, Jesus, as a manufacturer might, after a succession of defective doorknobs, hit upon the right formula and come up with a perfect doorknob. "The essential difference," McCabe writes,

is that each doorknob is a separate thing; it exists by itself and does not depend for its existence on its relationship to other doorknobs. The manufacture of doorknobs is just the making of one example after another, each one an isolated entity, whereas the making of men is the making of mankind; a man exists in his relationships to others. The perfect man, then, the being that man was meant to be, cannot be just an individual example of the human race; his perfection will consist in his setting up a new kind of relationship with the rest of mankind.[13]

He then continues:

To be a man is to be a centre of society, it is to be in communication with other men. . . . The imperfect man is the center of a limited society, his capacity for communication is exhausted by this society and supported by a hostility to others. I mean that each of us finds himself, finds his identity, in the centre of our group of friends or fellow-countrymen or whatever. A social grouping is constituted by

the overlapping social worlds of its members.
Because they overlap there is a common
world. This world is held together mainly by
the common ties between its members but
there is also the important external factor of
exclusiveness. It is held together not only by
love but also by fear; one of its bonds is a
common hostility to what is alien. This is
quite a common feature of other animal
societies. . . . The claim that Jesus is perfectly
human is the claim that his social world is
coextensive with humanity, that he is open to
all men and moreover open to all that is in
man. It is not just that he would like us to be
or that he proposes this as an ideal . . . but
that he actually is; the communication he offers is unmixed with domination or exclusiveness. So the coming of Jesus would be not
just the coming of an individual specimen of
the excellent or virtuous man, a figure whom
we might try to imitate, but the coming of a
new humanity, a new kind of community
among men. For this reason we can compare
the coming of Jesus to the coming of a new
language; and indeed, John does this: Jesus is
the word, the language of God which comes to
be a language for man.[14]

McCabe, I am convinced, is on to something of
tremendous significance for us in our effort to understand ourselves as moral beings and Jesus as the one
who is the way, the truth, and the light. Men live in
communities because their existence is inescapably a
co-existence, their being a being with. In company
with their fellows they seek to make for themselves
the "good" life, to secure those real goods that, together, perfect them as men because they correspond

to needs rooted in man's being. There is no need here to attempt to compile a catalog of these real goods perfective of human beings;[15] among them we would surely count life itself, health, truth, friendship, justice. All these goods are real goods; each is a good *of* man, not *for* man; each is a good to be *prized,* not *priced.* These goods, which are constitutive of the *bonum humanum,* define aspects of our personality, of our being. In addition, and this is exceedingly important, they are common goods insofar as they are not *my* goods or *your* goods in any exclusive sense but are rather human personal goods capable of being communicated to and shared by every human being.[16] Because they are real goods corresponding to needs existing in every human being just because he is human, they generate real rights; each human being has a claim on them, a right to them, precisely because he is a human being and because they are the realities that make a human being more human.[17] It is because of this that every human being is not only a moral being but is a being of moral worth. Each of us is, as an *individual* human being, a part of a larger whole, of the society of which we are members and in which we "grow" in our humanity; but each of us is, as an individual *human* or *moral* being, related to this society not simply as a part to a whole but as a whole to a whole. By this I mean that every human being, because he is a moral entity and a being of moral worth, has moral rights that are his because of what he is. It is for this reason that we abhor totalitarianism, which would subordinate individual human beings completely to the good of the state (i.e., those in power) and crush their rights in order to achieve goals worthwhile in themselves. Because men are moral beings, the common good of human societies must flow back to and be sharable by all the members of those societies.[18]

11

We come to know the goods constitutive of the *bonum humanum* and to love them in the communities of which we are a part. And these goods that we love and the persons in whom they are incarnated that we love form the focus of our existence. And here is the rub! Our love for these goods and for those human beings with whom we share our lives and goods and hopes, while binding us together as a community wherein we find our own identity, keeps us apart from the stranger, the alien, the foreigner. We fear him; we are afraid that he and his comrades will rob us of the goods to which *we* have a right, forgetting that he and his have just as much a claim on these goods as we do. We hate him, we close our heart to him and stop our ears so that we cannot listen to his cries for help. We foolishly, though understandably, refuse to recognize his humanity and that of his comrades, deeming ourselves and our loved ones "more" or "better" men than they. We reject the notion that the goods we love are his goods too and that the persons he loves and for whom he wills these goods are equally men as are the persons we love and for whom we will these goods. We reject his humanity because he is not one of us, because he is Jewish or Negro or Oriental or White or poor or stupid or mean—or unborn. Yes, we love the *bonum humanum* and the men for whom the *bonum humanum* exists, only we are quite selective in judging whom we shall count as men.

What Jesus tells us, and tells us even more by his being and his deeds than by his words, is that in rejecting the stranger, the alien, the "other" because he is "other" we are really rejecting ourselves and our own identity, our own humanity. He is telling us that we are denying, by our deeds that communicate ourselves and disclose our identity, our own drive to become fully human, for we can become fully human only if we accept our own humanity, as he did. He is telling us that we can fully accept our own humanity only if we are ready to accept the humanity of every man we meet, whether he is friend or foe, fellow intellectual or stupid adolescent, avant-garde Catholic or devotee of Frank Morriss.

Here it is instructive to note that the direction in which we have been led by reflecting on McCabe's way of expressing the human perfection of Jesus seems to converge with lines developing from the thought of contemporary moral philosophers and theologians and the great systematic theologian, Karl Rahner. To take the moral philosophers and moral theologians first. Despite differences, such moralists as Mortimer Adler, Germain Grisez, Josef Fuchs, Bruno Schüller, and Richard McCormick agree that the *bonum humanum* is, as indicated previously, pluriform, i.e., composed of individual real goods that, together, go to make up the good of man. They regard these real goods (e.g., life, health, justice) as "nonmoral" or "premoral" goods, and their destruction is what can be called "nonmoral" or "premoral" evil or *evil* as distinguished from *wickedness*. Morality, or, better, our identity as moral beings, enters in when we consider our *attitudes* toward these premoral goods and our way of pursuing them. To regard them as ours, and ours alone, is wicked; to pursue them and, in their pursuit, to be willing to destroy them in others is wicked, because this shows that we are willing to hate them in others and that we are open to their realization only in ourselves.[19] And to look on these goods in this way and to seek them in this way means, ultimately, that we are simply not ready to grant that other men have the same claim to them that we do; yet they do have this claim, and they have it for the same reason that we do, namely because they are human beings. What these moralists are saying, in other words, is that wickedness stems from our "heart," from the core of our being. It springs from a heart that is hardened against the claims of other men, that refuses to recognize them as being men on the same footing as ourselves.

Rahner's approach puts the focus somewhat differently, but what he has to say seems to me to be another line of thought converging with that taken by McCabe and with that taken by the moral philosophers and theologians just considered. Rahner's point is that a full acceptance of our own humanity is possible only if we accept the humanity of others, and that acceptance of the humanity of our fellowmen is implicitly an acceptance of Christ and of the Father who sent him.[20] And, it must also be noted, the capacity fully to accept our own humanity is a capacity that is ours only because there is a God who loves us and who has othered himself to become one with us and who summons us to his own life.[21]

Possibly the matter could be put this way. As the one who opens our eyes to a new mode of communication, Jesus is telling us that we are, as linguistic and moral beings, *responsive* beings.[22] Human communication through speech and action implies that human existence is to be a dialogue, not a monologue. In a dialogue one person addresses another, and the other replies or responds. Our being as moral beings, in short, is dialogical, and this means, literally, *through a word*. If we now look on human existence in this way and reflect on this existence as Christians, i.e., as those who believe that Jesus is the Father's Word to men, we will soon see that all men are, in a very real sense, "words" addressed to other men by their loving Father. We are the created words that the Uncreated Word became. To be a man, to be a human being, to be a moral being, then, is to be that being whom God himself, as Rahner puts it, "becomes (though remaining God) when he exteriorizes himself into the dimension of what is other than himself, the non-divine."[23] To be a man, then, is to be that being that "ensues when God's self-utterance, his Word, is given out lovingly into the void of god-less nothing."[24] Man, in short, is the "code-word" for God, and the living God of history, the God who "othered" himself in Jesus of Nazareth, is to be discovered "precisely where we are, and can only be found there."[25] Put another way, we can say that man's existence, as disclosed to us in Jesus, is the ultimate reason why there is the divine command not to make graven images. The reason is simply that God has already made his image, and this image is man, who is his living ikon, an ikon that God himself became in Jesus.

In our struggle to find ourselves, to discover our identity, to fulfill our destiny, moreover, we need help. Our moral lives are not lived in some kind of vacuum, and to do what we know to be the right thing, the "human" thing, we need help and support. This is a point brought home graphically to us by a passage in St. Paul's letter to the Romans, where he writes: "I do not understand my own actions. For I do not do what I want, but I do the very thing I hate. . . . I can will what is right, but I cannot do it. For I do not do the good I want, but the evil that I do not want is what I do" (Romans 7:15-19).

Something paradoxical, indeed something indicative of the depths of man's existence, is at stake here. The paradox can only make sense if we admit that there are operative in human existence factors that John Macquarrie has called *enabling* or supportive and *disabling* or destructive.[26] We do not "pull ourselves up by our own bootstraps," as it were. We do not live as isolated entities totally autonomous and independent in our actions, but in a real world where our lives, thoughts, and deeds are woven into the fabric of a corporate or social context. To discover who we are and what we are to do if we are to become human in the second or normative sense and to be able to do what we know truly must be done, we need support, we need help. But too frequently in place of support we find ourselves, as did Paul, impotent or powerless. We are affected by disabling or crippling factors over which, seemingly, we have no control. We live, in short, in a world of tension between sin and grace, between disabling factors and enabling factors.

The real world in which we struggle to become human is a world, it must be acknowledged, that has been wounded by sin, by man's failure to respond in trust and love to the words uttered to him by his Father, and uttered to him in the person of his fellowmen. Sin is a reality, and its reality has important repercussions on our struggle to do what we know is in truth the right or human thing to do (and this is a subject to which we must return later for closer reflection). But, as Macquarrie points out,[27] the world in which we live is a world in which grace is also operative and is, indeed, prior to sin. As Christians we know that the God we love and the God who loves us is an Emmanuel, a God who is, as Karl Barth has put it, "neither *next* to man nor *above* him, but *with* him, *by* him, and most important, *for* him."[28] Our God is the God who became one of us in Jesus. And this God is with us now, for Jesus *is,* and he is still man. Although many, infected by the docetist mentality mentioned at the beginning of this chapter, imagine that Jesus, after being raised from the dead, went back to being God again, our faith is that this man Jesus is still with us, is still one of us. As man he is still with us, present to us in our struggle to make

16

sense of our lives and in our efforts to discover our humanity, our identity. He is with us even if we refuse to recognize him, and he offers himself to us personally in the *zoa logika*, the *eikones theou*, the created words whom we meet in our daily lives and with whom we collaborate to achieve the human. We know this because he told us that in giving a cup of water to a stranger we are giving it to him. We know this because with Paul we believe that nothing, "neither angels nor principalities, neither the present nor the future, nor powers, neither height nor depth nor any other creature, will be able to separate us from the love of God that comes to us in Christ Jesus our Lord" (Romans 8:35-38).

III

Some comments on the relationship between Christian ethics and what was referred to earlier as the "moral strivings" of mankind (which would, of course, include the efforts that philosophers have made to understand man's existence as a moral being) seem appropriate before bringing this chapter to a close.[29] This is a question that has provoked serious thought and debate from the very early days of Christianity, and although it is not my purpose to explore this matter in any depth, it is purposeful to present some reflections.

A Christian ethics *is* different from any other kind of ethics. But what is the difference? Is there a total dichotomy or break between Christian ethics and the "moral strivings" of mankind, or is there a line of continuity? Although there has always been, within the Christian community, a tradition stressing the difference of Christian ethics to such a degree that there hardly seems any point of contact with non-Christian ethics—a tradition expressed in

Tertullian's famous statement "What has Jerusalem to do with Athens?," in the suspicion and distrust of the "natural" that is found in the major Protestant Reformers, and to some degree in the works of such contemporary writers as Karl Barth and Paul Lehmann—there has always been another tradition, one certainly reflected in the Catholic community, that Christian ethics, although distinctly different, stands in continuity with "natural" ethics. The precise character of this continuity, however, has been variously expressed, and the varied approaches to formulating this continuity of Christian ethics with the moral strivings of mankind are closely linked to the ways in which theologians have attempted to think about the process of man's redemption and the relationship between nature and grace, between the "natural" and the "supernatural."[30]

My purpose here is not to enter into an examination of this subject in all its ramifications, but simply to offer some observations that seem to flow from the position developed previously with respect to the character of human existence as a moral existence and the difference that Jesus makes. These observations, moreover, seem compatible with the efforts of theologians such as Karl Rahner,[31] Charles Curran,[32] and others to reformulate the question of man's salvation in Jesus and to rethink the character of the relationship between Christian ethics and the moral strivings of mankind.

From what we have said already, it should be apparent that the relationship between religion and morality, between Christian ethics and man's moral strivings, is *not* something accidental or extrinsic. It is not as though religion or Christian faith is outside of man's moral existence, an external support of this existence providing it with appropriate sanctions in the form of "rewards" and "punishments." Nor is it a

18

relationship that need be *consciously* recognized, as if a person could not be a moral being, could not become fully human unless he explicitly affirmed belief in God and in Christ. To regard the relationship between religion and morality, between a Christian ethics and man's moral being, in this way is, in fact, a serious threat to human existence in addition to being a terribly distorted understanding of this relationship. As Reinhold Niebuhr has noted, "there is no deeper pathos in the spiritual life of man than the cruelty of the righteous,"[33] and this is what results when people believe that human beings cannot be truly good unless they are Christians. Countless human beings have suffered enormously at the hand of those who confidently claimed to be God's emissaries, and history provides us with numerous examples of the ruthlessness of the righteous: the Inquisition, the Peasants' War, the Scopes trial, the terror in Northern Ireland and the tragedy of Bangladesh. Ludwig Feuerbach was surely correct when he observed that "wherever morality is based on theology, wherever the right is made dependent on divine authority, the most immoral, unjust, infamous things can be justified and established."[34]

In addition, to claim that a person can be morally good only if he is religious in the sense of being explicitly ready to acknowledge God and Christ is unrealistic. In fact, one of the major sources of embarrassment for religious people today is their discovery that "those who profess no religion at all are even more energetic than themselves in working for social justice and the achievement of a better life for mankind."[35] In fact, it can be truthfully said, as Knud Løgstrup, a Danish theologian puts it, that "the Christian faith does not endow a person with superior moral wisdom."[36] The Christian, it may be suggested, shares with all serious-minded people the same concern to do good and avoid evil, to build a better world, to do the "right" or "human" thing. He does not, simply because he is a Christian, enjoy an inside track, as it were, on the moral life. When it comes to making judgments about the rightness or wrongness of specific kinds of human activity, Christian ethics and "natural" ethics are in continuity, share a common ground. This ground is the lived experiences of human beings and the drive to understand these experiences and to verify the meaning they have for human existence.

Yet, as writers such as John Macquarrie and Charles Curran, among others, observe,[37] the person who is a Christian approaches the moral situations in which he must decide what he rightfully must do if he is to become human from a framework or perspective that differs from that of the non-Christian. His ultimate view, or what some writers have called "blik," of man's moral life is different. It is different because within the Christian community and, therefore, the individual Christian, there are *consciously articulated,* however dimly perceived, true meanings of human experience that, although present and operative in others, may be only pre-consciously or very obscurely recognized. The Christian is in a position, simply by reason of his being Christian, to grasp, dimly perhaps but nevertheless in a meaningful and unforgettable way, that his own destiny is inextricably intertwined with the destiny of others and that he can only become truly human in company with his fellows. He recognizes that the rights he has simply because he is a human being or a being of moral worth are rights that he possesses not for himself and his friends alone but *with* and *for* his fellowman, wherever he is present.[38] He is able to recognize in a conscious way that the mystery of human life is inseparable from the mystery of divine life and that

20

God's becoming man summons him to become fully man and thereby to live a life that God himself wills to share with him.

In one sense, then, we can say that Christian ethics is continuous with the moral strivings of mankind with respect to its concern to discover what it is that men must do if they are to make human life human, and that it is distinctive in that it provides a specific perspective for carrying out our endeavor to move from experience through understanding to truth and responsible action and for integrating all our understanding of ourselves and our moral lives into a broader vision of the meaning of human existence that results from our belief in God's saving deeds in our behalf in Jesus.

But there is more to the difference between a Christian ethics than this—at least I believe that there is and the nature of this difference will be more to the center of the stage at a later part in this work. Briefly put, it is this. Our moral lives, as noted previously, are lived out in a very real world, a world where we are both enabled and disabled in our struggle to discover who we are and what we are to do if we are to become who we are meant to be. We are enabled or disabled on two different levels, the one cognitive, the other conative, and these levels interpenetrate. We need help, in other words, both to come to know what we are to do and to be able to do what we know we are to do—and we can be crippled on each of these interpenetrating levels. The mission of the Christian community, of the assembly of those gathered in the name of the risen Jesus, is, at least in part, to provide for all men the supportive context that will enable them to come to know what is human and to do this. This mission too is central to a Christian ethics; it is a mission that it shares with ethics rooted in other human traditions and experiences, to be sure, but it is a mission so central and significant that it is a characteristic or defining feature of Christian ethics. It is a mission that, I believe, must be kept in mind as an undergirding element in the discussions to follow and one that demands investigation as such when we come to consider the existential context of our moral lives.

This chapter is a revision of my paper, "Jesus as the Presence of God in Our Moral life," in *Does Jesus Make a Difference?* edited by Thomas M. McFadden (New York: Seabury, 1974), the Proceedings of the College Theology Society. I am grateful to Dr. McFadden for permission to use this material.

Notes

1. This is the approach taken by Charles E. Curran, among others, in his "The Central Message of Jesus: Conversion," in *A New Look at Christian Morality* (Notre Dame, Ind.: Fides, 1968).

2. For a scholarly study of these approaches to Jesus and our moral lives see James Gustafson, *Christ and Our Moral Life* (New York: Harper & Row, 1968).

3. René Dubos, *So Human an Animal* (New York: Random House, 1969).

4. Jean-Paul Sartre, *Being and Nothingness,* trans. Hazel Barnes (New York: Philosophical Library, 1956), p. 615.

5. Bernard J. F. Lonergan, *Method in Theology* (New York: Herder & Herder, 1972), p. 18.

6. *Ibid.,* p. 11.

7. Herbert McCabe, *What Is Ethics All About?* (Washington: Corpus, 1969), pp. 18-19.

8. Lonergan, *op. cit.,* pp. 20-25.

9. The fact that we live in a world not of pure, immediate experience, but in a world where experience is mediated to us by meaning assumes critical importance in the process of humanization or of socialization. This subject will be explored from a different perspective in the subsequent chapter; here it ought to be noted that the philosophical views of Lonergan seem to parallel in a remarkable way the positions reached by empirical sociological research in the work of Peter Berger and others.

10. McCabe, *op. cit.*, p. 68.

11. Here too it is worth noting that McCabe's analysis of the way men "grow" into their world by adapting to the linguistic systems of the communities of which they are members parallels the views of Berger and others. Of this more in the subsequent chapter.

12. McCabe, *op. cit.*, pp. 74-75.

13. *Ibid.*, pp. 127-128.

14. *Ibid.*, pp. 128-129.

15. An excellent commentary on this subject is provided by Germain G. Grisez, *Abortion: The Myths, the Realities, and the Arguments* (New York: Corpus, 1970), Chapter Six.

16. On this see Jacques Maritain, *The Person and the Common Good* (New York: Charles Scribner's Sons, 1947), Chapter Two.

17. On this see Mortimer Adler, *The Time of Our Lives: The Ethics of Common Sense* (New York: Holt, Rinehart, and Winston, 1971), Chapter Six.

18. On this see Maritain, *op. cit.*, Chapter Two, and also Paul Ramsey, *The Just War* (New York: Charles Scribner's Sons, 1968), Chapter One.

19. On this see Grisez, *op. cit.*, p. 312, ff. On the views of Schüller and Fuchs see Richard A. McCormick, "Notes on Moral Theology," *Theological Studies* 32 (1972) 68-72.

20. Karl Rahner, "Jesus Christ," *Sacramentum Mundi* (New York: Herder & Herder, 1969) 3, 194.

21. *Ibid.*

22. An excellent study of the theme of responsibility in contemporary religious ethics is Albert Jonsen's *Responsibility in Modern Religious Ethics* (Washington: Corpus, 1968). Jonsen studies this theme as it has been developed in the writings of Dietrich Bonhoeffer, H. Richard Niebuhr, Robert Johann, and Bernard Häring.

23. Rahner, "On the Theology of the Incarnation," *Theological Investigations* (Baltimore: Helicon, 1966), 4, 113.

24. *Ibid.*, p. 116.

25. *Ibid.*

26. John Macquarrie, *Three Issues in Ethics* (New York: Harper & Row, 1970), pp. 119-125. This chapter from Macquarrie's book has recently been reprinted in a very worthwhile anthology edited by C. Ellis Nelson, *Conscience: Theological and Psychological Perspectives* (New York: Paulist, 1973).

27. *Ibid.*, p. 122.

28. Karl Barth, *Introduction to Evangelical Theology* (New York: Holt, Rinehart, and Winston, 1963), p. 11.

29. Some recent works that discuss this topic in a stimulating way are the following: John Macquarrie, *Three Issues in Ethics* (New York: Harper & Row, 1970); Charles E. Curran, *Catholic Moral Theology in Dialoque* (Notre Dame, Ind.: Fides, 1972), Chapter One, "Dialogue With Humanism,"; and G. N. A. Robinson, *The Groundwork of Christian Ethics* (Philadelphia: Westminster, 1972).

30. A concise and perceptive survey of this question is given in Gustavo Gutierrez, *A Theology of Liberation* (Maryknoll, N.Y.: Orbis Books, 1973), pp. 63-78.

31. See in particular his *Hearers of the Word* (New York: Herder & Herder, 1967).

32. Curran, *op. cit.*, Chapter One. In a very suggestive passage Curran proposes that we substitute th expression "human experience" for "nature" and notes that human experience was the focal point for the pastoral theology of Vatican II. Unfortunately he does not develop the theme in depth.

33. Reinhold Niebuhr, *An Interpretation of Christian Ethics* (New York: Meridian, 1956), p. 203.

34. Ludwig Feuerbach, *The Essence of Christianity*, trans. George Eliot (New York: Harper Torchbooks), p. 274. On this subject it is instructive to read the masterful "Legend of the Grand Inquisitor" in Dostoevski's *The Brothers Karamazov*.

35. Robert Johann, *The Pragmatic Meaning of God* (Milwaukee: Marquette University Press, 1966), p. 17.

36. Knud Løgstrup, *The Ethical Demand*, trans. Theodore Jensen (Philadelphia: Fortress Press, 1971), p. 127.

37. See material cited in note 29 above.

38. On this see Paul Ramsey, *The Christian and the Sit-in* (New York: Association Press, 1966), p. 78.

Chapter Two:

KNOWING THE HUMAN

How do we get to know the human? How can we discern what is human in the normative sense and thus come to know what it is that we are to do if we are to answer the summons to become more fully human? This is an exceptionally difficult question, and because of the very real difficulty in answering it many have concluded that it is unanswerable or even that it is absurd or meaningless or, at the most, strictly contingent on the type of culture or socialization to which we are exposed.

In this chapter our purpose is to explore this question and to do so, first, by looking into the matter primarily from the perspective of philosophical analysis—although, as we shall discover, the work of cultural anthropologists and psychologists is particularly pertinent—and, second, from the viewpoint of sociologists who have been concerned with the way in which human beings become acclimatized, as it were, and discover their identity in the communities in which they live.

I

John Dewey once remarked that "at some place on

the globe, at some time, every kind of practice seems to have been tolerated or even praised."[1] This statement, and it is one that can be supported by historians and cultural anthropologists, serves to make us aware of an important fact of human experience, namely that men differ enormously in their ways of evaluating human deeds, practices, and institutions, in their appraisals of what it means to be "human" in the second or normative sense. Activities and practices regarded with disgust by one group of human beings may be highly esteemed by others, and it is very easy to point out specific examples such as slavery, torture, cannibalism, infanticide, polygamy, premarital intercourse, homosexual relations. This fact was illustrated in a striking way when a group of Palestinian terrorists seized Israeli athletes competing at the Munich Olympics in the summer of 1972, held them as hostages, and eventually slaughtered them when an effort to rescue them failed. Most of the world reacted in outrageous horror at the deed, condemning it as an act of atrocious inhumanity. The terrorists, nevertheless, were seen as heroes in many parts of the Arab world and their deed was not only condoned but glorified.

Because contradictory evaluations of human behavior are so widespread and are apparently indicative of the human condition some have concluded that it is impossible to make any "objectively" true judgments about the meaning of the human in its normative sense. Many would agree with the noted anthropologist Ruth Benedict that to say that something is morally right or good, i.e., normatively human, is simply to say that it is "customary." For these persons, no one value system is any better than any other, no given practice or institution is inherently better than its contradictory. On this view the only persons qualified to pass judgment on activities and practices are persons within the cultural group wherein the activities and practices make sense.[2]

The problems that this fact of ethical diversity poses must be faced honestly by anyone interested in discovering what it is that makes and keeps human life human. Yet there are ways of interpreting this fact—meanings attributed to it—that destroy, for all practical purposes, the entire effort to discover the meaning or significance of man's moral strivings and that reduce ethics to a simple description of the way people actually behave, eviscerating human activities of any significance or intelligibility.

One interpretation of the fact of ethical diversity is expressed in Montaigne's famous saying, echoed by Shakespeare, that "nothing is either good or bad but thinking makes it so,"[3] or in the frequently voiced expression that "one man's meat is another man's poison." On this interpretation everything is relative *in the sense that everything is arbitrary,* that is, up to the choice or preference of the individual or group concerned. If this view is true, it follows that nothing that we can discover in the way things are, in the relationships that exist in and among human beings, can help us tell whether specifiable kinds of acts or practices or institutions are right or wrong, capable of furthering or hindering the process of humanization. Rightness and wrongness are *not,* on this view, rooted in reality, intelligently discernible in the real relations that are set up in and through human deeds. Rather they are exclusively and totally dependent on the way men think and/or feel. In other words, on this view we do not *discover* anything of human or moral significance in our activities but rather *impose* this significance on our activities. To rape a twelve-year-old girl or to tear the tongue out of a six-year-old for "lying," on this view, would be wrong not because of

27

anything this act tells us about the human beings involved but only because some people *think* or *opine* or *feel* that this is wrong. To throw oneself on a live grenade that has landed in a crowd of people in order to save them would be heroic or courageous, on this view, not because of anything humanly intelligible in the deed and all that it involves, but solely because most men would *declare* that an act of this kind is heroic or courageous. And so it is with everything else that men do—with being loyal to a friend or betraying him, with paying a living wage to one's employees or exploiting the powerless and ignorant.

Closely allied to this subjective, arbitrary way of deciding what is human and what is not is the view that ethical or value judgments are in no way expressions of what we know or can come to know but are only emotional or rhetorical utterances. This view has been set forth quite straightforwardly by several thinkers, among them David Hume in the eighteenth century[4] and A. J. Ayer, Hume's disciple in many ways, in ours. The latter, for example, writes:

Fundamental ethical concepts are unanalyz-able, inasmuch as there is no criterion by which we can test the validity of the judgments in which they occur. . . . The reason why they are unanalyzable is that they are mere pseudo-concepts. The presence of an ethical symbol in a proposition adds nothing to its factual content. Thus if I say to someone, "You acted wrongly in stealing that money," I am not stating anything more than if I had simply said, "You stole that money" in a peculiar tone of horror, or written it with the addition of some special exclamation marks. . . . If now I generalize my previous statement and say, "Stealing money is wrong," I produce a sentence which has no factual meaning—that is, expresses no proposition which can be either true or false.[5]

For Hume, Ayer, and those who share their views, consequently, it is meaningless to ask about the truth of any ethical or value judgment, of any statement that seeks to specify what we mean by the human. Since these statements are not expressions of any kind of knowledge in their view but simply display the emotional reaction or feelings of the person or persons making them, they cannot be true nor can they be false. They can be called true or false only to the extent that they accurately reflect or fail to reflect our inner feelings, not in the sense that they express anything intelligibly discoverable in the activities and events to which we respond emotionally.

The position championed by Hume and Ayer, it should be noted, brings to the fore, in addition to the fact of widespread diversity and disagreement in moral practices, another consideration that seems to support a relativistic view of morality or appraisal of the human in its normative sense. They stress the difference between factual or descriptive statements and moral or value statements. For them, and for those who agree with them, factual or descriptive statements—*is* statements—can be verified or falsified by observation, by making tests of various sorts. Moral or value statements—*ought* statements—on the other hand, such as "it is wrong to barbecue neonates in order to advance scientific knowledge," or "one ought not to tear the tongue out of six-year-old children to punish them for lying," cannot be verified or falsified by some kind of experiment or observation.

A skeptical and relativistic attitude toward moral values, consequently, seems to be supported by two major kinds of consideration, the one factual, the other logical or linguistic. Although we cannot deny the fact that men do differ, and differ enormously, in their opinions about the humanness or inhumanness of specific sorts of acts and practices, we can advance many important reasons to show that this fact does not warrant a mordant skepticism and cynical relativism—or what some might term a humane tolerance or an openmindedness—with respect to moral questions. I believe, incidentally (although this is an important incidental), that the issue is not so much between *relativism* and *absolutism* as it is between *extrinsicism* and *intrinsicism*. If one scratches a relativist deeply enough (as we shall soon see), he will discover that the relativist does have *his* absolutes, as does every human being (after all, to say that *everything is relative* is to say that one thing, at least, is absolute, namely, that everything is relative). But the core of the relativistic mentality is that the value-making factor, the right-making factor, the human-making factor in any moral situation, is something that is *extrinsic to* or *outside of* the moral situation itself.[6] It resides in the "thinking" (Montaigne) or opining or evaluating of the person and/or groups involved or in their emotions (Hume, Ayer) or responses to the situation. One who opposes relativism in ethics is asserting primarily that the value-making factor/factors is/are rooted within the moral situation itself. In other words, for the relativist something is right (human, valuable) *because* it is thought to be such or opined to be such or responded to as such. For the non-relativist, on the contrary, one judges or opines or responds to something as valuable because it *is* so. The non-relativist is aware that one's judgment or opinion or response may be erroneous but maintains that it is corrigible, at least in principle if not existentially, for this person

30

or group of persons, and affirms that the rightness or wrongness (the humanness or inhumanness) of a deed or practice or institution depends on intelligibly discoverable reality-making factors rooted in the moral situation, not on the fallible human judgments or opinions or responses to the moral situation.

But what about the fact that men do differ tremendously in their ways of evaluating or appraising human behavior? Here it ought first of all to be noted that a conflict between different groups of human beings or between different individuals about the rightness or wrongness of a given mode of behavior may *not* indicate a fundamental or basic disagreement over a moral value. Richard B. Brandt, for instance, in a very informative article on the question of ethical relativity, makes the following observation:

it is not necessarily a case of fundamental disagreement in values if one group approves of children's executing their parents at a certain age or stage of feebleness whereas another group disapproves of this very strongly. It may be that in the first group the act is thought necessary for the welfare of the parents in the afterlife, whereas in the second group it is thought not to be. The disagreement might well be removed by agreement about the facts, and indeed both parties might subscribe, now, to the principle, "It is right for a child to treat a parent in whatever way is required for the parent's long-range welfare." The disagreement might be simply about the implications of this common principle, in the light of differing conceptions of the facts. [7]

It is possible that many factual instances of disagreement or conflict over moral issues could be explained in this way. Many practices, deemed good and human by individuals and societies, are seen in much different light if new evidence is brought forward, if the persons involved are exposed to new kinds of experience, if questions are raised about the meaning that has been formulated with respect to some aspect of human experience. Still it must be admitted that societies and individuals disagree vehemently, even violently, about the rightness or wrongness of given acts and practices, even when they may agree about the facts involved. But does this fact support the position of ethical relativism, are other alternative explanations or interpretations more adequate? Several lines of argument and evidence can be advanced to show that ethical relativism cannot be the correct interpretation of experience.

One counterargument that focuses on some negative considerations is that ethical relativism inevitably leads to living contradictions. For instance, to say, with Montaigne, that "nothing is either good or bad but thinking makes it so," or to agree with Ruth Benedict's assertion that all value systems are equally valid and must be tolerated is to take a position that ends up in existential absurdities. If something is good, valuable, human in the normative sense *only* because it is *thought* to be good or *declared* to be good by particular groups or individuals—and this basically is what Montaigne, Benedict, and other relativists are saying—then it follows that all value systems are not only equally valuable but also equally valueless, and this is patently absurd. The self-defeating character of a purely relativist position has been illustrated in a persuasive way by Henry Veatch, a professor of philosophy at Georgetown University. Professor Veatch compared the views of two publicly acknowledged relativists, Ruth Benedict and Benito Mussolini, to make his point. Both Benedict and Mussolini agree that moral values—the "human" in the normative sense—are relative, that is, dependent upon the "thinking" or opinions of various groups or individuals. But both, beginning with the same relativistic suppositions, reached contradictory conclusions. Ruth Benedict argued that the equal validity of all value systems should lead us (note the "value" character of her conclusion) to respect the values of others, especially when these conflict with our own. She argued, quite inconsistently for a relativist, that one value—that of tolerance—is really or absolutely or independently valuable, and with this as her independent or inherent value she claimed that we have a moral obligation to be tolerant of the values of others. (Note that everyone, it seems, has some absolutes, and these function either implicitly or explicitly in his arguments. This is itself of interest, for the value that is regarded as an absolute is undoubtedly, as we shall be seeing later, something genuinely important for men, something really good for men, a component of the *bonum humanum.*) Mussolini, on the contrary, concluded, that the equal validity or invalidity of all value systems meant that his preferred value (the one that functioned as an absolute in *his* mind), namely the right of the stronger to impose their will on the weaker by force, is just as valuable as tolerance and that no one has the right to prevent the stronger from not tolerating the values of the weaker. In other words, as Veatch points out, both Benedict and Mussolini are saying, in effect, the same thing: "Since no course of action is really better or superior to any other, I conclude that the better course of action for me to follow would be thus and so,"[8] that is, in the case of Benedict to practice tolerance and in the case of Mussolini to impose my will on others by force.

Proceeding from negative counterindications to more positive or constructive ways of coping with the fact that men do differ widely in their value judgments, it is possible to examine closely the factual and logical considerations that give rise to relativism. First we can look at the *factual* basis of relativism, a basis stressed by writers like Benedict, Karl Westermarck, and others. From the *fact* that men do disagree tremendously about value judgments, these writers concluded that the reason why this disagreement exists is that values are dependent on factors *extrinsic to* human deeds, practices, and institutions. Non-relativists agree about the fact requiring explanation, but deny that factual considerations compel one to conclude that all values (goods, the "human") are the creations of cultures. Indeed, the non-relativist can argue that an examination of facts (human experiences) will show that although not all values are universal, that is, respected by and appealing to all men, *some* universal values are discovered. For instance, recent empirical studies conducted by Lawrence Kohlberg and his associates into the development of moral awareness and reasoning in adolescents show that "basic moral values are universal," in the sense that they are transcultural and operative in all human communities.[9] Kohlberg's investigations, which centered on the logical structure of the arguments and reasons that adolescents of varying cultural backgrounds advanced to support their solutions to moral dilemmas, showed that certain key moral concepts—among them such value concepts as life, justice, human welfare—were operative universally. Kohlberg's conclusions were (1) that moral values—what I have termed previously basic human goods genuinely constitutive of the *bonum humanum*—function as *principles or modes of choosing* (a point to which we shall return later) and (2) that the marked differences in the value or moral judgments and customs that exist between individuals and cultures are to be explained, not by ethical relativity, but by the differences in the stage or developmental status of the individuals and cultures in question.[10] His research, which has been going on for more than fourteen years, provides empirical evidence to support the non-relativist position that basic human goods or values are dependent on reality-making or truth-making factors rooted in the "way things are" and are *not* the products or creations of individual minds or cultures. The specific ways in which these values or goods (e.g., life, justice, human welfare) are protected and pursued *are*, however, culturally conditioned; and the way that they function concretely in moral argumentation depends on the developmental status of the individuals and cultures concerned. But their *reality* is transcultural.

The results of Kohlberg's studies are remarkable, but they ought not to be too surprising. For it is a fact that all men, whether they are Eskimos, Samoan Islanders, Australian aborigines, denizens of Watergate in either its physical or symbolic sense, are human beings. As human beings they are biologically a community. All men, simply because they are men, are linked to one another. Our being as humans is a *being with*, human existence is a co-existence. Our being is, in other words, relational in the sense that our being as humans actually consists in large measure *in* our relationships to our fellowmen. As members of the one human race we are not linked together as units of a logical class, for instance the class of all red objects, but are rather inextricably linked to one another as members of the same living species. And this is critically important for our identity and for our identity as *moral* beings. The importance of this distinction between being a member of a logical class and being a member of a living species is graphically described in the following passage from Herbert McCabe:

Mankind is not just a logical class but a species, constituted by relationships amongst its members. There is such an identifiable object as the species of panthers to which all panthers belong; there is no such object as the 'class of all red things' to which all red things belong. To say 'this belongs to the class of red things' is just a pompous way of saying 'this is red.' It adds absolutely nothing to what you know of an individual red thing to be told that it belongs to such a class. But 'this belongs to the species of panther' is a remark different from, and more informative than, 'this is a panther.' You might say the latter without realizing there existed a species of panthers. . . . To be told that it belongs to a species is to be told not that there are others like it (there may not be; perhaps they have all been shot), but that part of what this panther is is to be a fragment of a larger whole. It is to be told that part of its behaviour is to be explained by the requirements of this larger whole. Not to know that the panther belongs to a species would be not to know something about this individual panther; membership of the species is part of what it means for the panther to be itself. It is a consequence of this that when its behaviour is influenced by its membership of the species, it is not suffering violence from outside. There may well be a tension between what it would like to do as an individual and what it has to do as a species-member, but this is a tension within the animal itself. When it acts in accordance with the inhibition, let us say, it is not submitting to some exterior force, but to a depth within itself.[11]

Because man is a being-with-others who discovers his identity in the common struggle of mankind to find ways for making life livable, for making human life human, it follows that the goods perfective of man are not purely individual goods. Basic human goods, in other words, are not *my* goods or *your* goods, but human goods. They are goods of all men just because they are men. They are goods *of* men, not *for* men; and they are goods, as we have already noted, that are sharable, communicable. These goods, moreover, correspond to *needs* that exist with us just because we are the kind of beings that we are. They are correlated to inclinations or tendencies that are rooted in us just because we are members of the species, man. By reason of our membership of a particular species of animal life, and by reason of the fact that our animality differs from the animality of other animals because we are the linguistic, inquiring, questioning beings that we are, we have specifiable needs or inclinations, correlating to these needs are certain kinds of realities that we call goods. These goods that are basic to our existence as human beings comprise, together, the *bonum humanum*. These realities are good or valuable for human beings not because human beings *think* that they are such but because they really are, and our thinking is true when we truthfully identify these goods.

Perhaps the point that I am trying to make here will become clearer if we relate the work of a contemporary moral philosopher, Germain Grisez, who works out of a Christian context, to the empirical researches of Professor Kohlberg. Grisez, philosophically in the Thomistic tradition of natural law, draws on the writings of such psychologists as Ernest Hilgard[12] and such anthropologists as Robert H. Lowie[13] to show that all men, simply because they are men, have certain basic needs or inclinations. These needs are not, of course, consciously known to us when we are born. But by reflecting on our experience, by asking questions of it, we can discover these needs and objectify them in our consciousness. The process Grisez describes, it ought also to be noted, seems accurately to reflect the dynamism that Lonergan has in mind when he writes about our spontaneous movement from experiencing to understanding to truth to responsible action.[14] Although it may not be possible, as Grisez suggests,[15] to enumerate all of man's basic needs or inclinations and the goods corresponding to them, or to formulate them properly—for, after all, we are constantly enlarging our horizons through new experiences and through new kinds of questions that become meaningful because of our experiences - it is certainly possible to affirm that some realities (goods) do correspond to genuine or basic human needs. Among these we would include—and strikingly this is exactly what Kohlberg discovered in his empirical studies—such goods as life itself, including health, justice, friendship, knowledge, etc. These goods or realities are what some writers, as we have previously noted, call "premoral" or "nonmoral" goods. Together they make up the *bonum humanum* or the human good. Each is a real good; each corresponds to a real need that we have as human beings; each marks off, as it were, a dimension of our personality, of our being. None totally exhausts the *bonum humanum*, the full range of the good possible for man, so that none is an absolute in the sense that it is the be-all and the end-all of human existence. But none, on the other hand, is arbitrarily good, good only because it is opined or judged to be good or valuable. None is relative in this sense, and none is so relative that it can be ridden over as of no significance. Each, in other words, claims to be recognized for what it is, a real good of human beings, a good that is to be prized not priced, a good that corresponds to real needs that human beings have, a good that opens up possibilities for human existence.

Moreover, and here too there is a striking convergence between what Grisez and other writers in his tradition and Kohlberg have to say, each of these goods *as consciously known* functions as a *purposeful motive for our behavior*. These goods, as Grisez writes, are to be pursued in our actions "not because any external authority imposes them but because we must pursue some good if intelligently guided action is to be possible at all."[16] In other words, these goods, as consciously known and as objectified in our knowledge, provide us with what Grisez, following his scholastic tradition, calls "principles of practical reason,"[17] or what we might term "principles of intelligent activity." Their *function* is precisely the function that Kohlberg discovers operative in the basic values (goods) that he believes, as a result of his empirical investigations, are universally common to all men, for in Kohlberg's view basic moral principles, which articulate basic values, are "universal mode(s) of a choosing . . . general guide(s) to choice."[18] The basic human goods or values, in other words, provide us with the basic principles that make our choices intelligible or understandable. They do *not*, and this is extremely important and is something explicitly recognized by both Grisez and Kohlberg, suffice to tell us whether any specific action or practice is right or wrong (human or inhuman)—that is something that is to be determined by reality- or truth-making factors that show how and to what extent our love for these basic human goods is embodied in our actions or not, and is a subject to which we shall return later—but they do give us the intelligible justifications or reasons or warrants for the choices that we make. No matter what we choose to do, whether it is indeed "right" or "human" or "wrong" or "inhuman," when we seek to defend our course of action and to persuade others of its rightness, we appeal to one or the other of these basic human goods. Their reality is the root reason why a relativistic, skeptical, subjective appraisal of morality and of the rightness or wrongness of human deeds is erroneous. And in fact, as Kohlberg's research indicates, these goods are true human goods of all human beings. They are the goods, as Mortimer Adler notes, that generate real rights for human beings. Every human being, precisely because he is not an isolated entity but is indeed a member of the species man, has a claim on these goods, for they correspond to needs that he has because he is the kind of being that he is.[19]

These goods are not abstractions or intelligible principles—as consciously understood and articulated, of course, they generate principles—but are perfections subsisting in real human beings. From a religious perspective we can say that the morally good person—the one whose heart is clean, the one who, like the good tree, bears good fruit—is the man who is *open* to these goods and their realization in all men. He is the one who recognizes that these goods are goods of all men, not his or his friends' exclusively. He is the one who, in Rahner's terms, is open to his own humanity and who is thus open to God and Christ.

Earlier it was noted that ethical relativism, in addition to appealing to facts for support, also offers logical or linguistic arguments. The later, as advanced by Ayer and others, hold that it is not possible to describe value judgments (statements wherein we declare that something is morally right or wrong, that something is truly good or not for men) as either true or false. This contention is valid only if one accepts the particular theory regarding meaningfully true propositions common to these writers. For them only two kinds of statements or propositions can be meaningful in the sense that they can properly be called true or false. The first type are analytical or apriori propositions whose truth is not dependent on empirical, observable evidence. These would include, for them, statements of identity such as "A is A" or "a rose is a rose" and statements in which the predicate is included in the definition of the subject, such as "lead is a fusible metal." The second type includes aposteriori or synthetic propositions whose truth depends on empirical evidence and is subject to verification or falsification by the observation of facts.

This theory, as Adler and others have noted, is simply defective as a general theory of propositions that can properly be said to be true or false.[20] On the level of analytic propositions, it completely ignores a third group of propositions or statements, in addition to statements of identity and definitions, that are expressive of truth. They are statements that older philosophers, among them Aristotle and Thomas Aquinas, called *truths of simple intelligence* and what Adler terms *truths of understanding*. A truth of understanding, such as "the whole is greater than any of its parts," "being is not non-being," " the one is not the many," and so forth, is neither a statement of identity (a whole is not a part nor is being non-being) nor a definition (a part is not an element in the definition of a whole nor is non-being part of the definition of being), for in strict reality there are no simpler terms in which realities of this kind can be explained. They are indefinable, but not unintelligible. Nor are these truths dependent upon empirical tests for verification; they depend on experience and reflection on experience (Lonergan's drive to understand by questioning experience) in order to become consciously articulated in our minds, but they are not "facts" or "data" that demand explanation; rather they are the bedrock of reality as intelligently discernible in virtue of which we are capable of making sense of any facts or data.

These truths are understood by us when we see how they are related to what the philosophers noted previously call their "commensurate universals," that is, when we understand the meaning of the realities that we relate to one another in propositions expressive of a truth of understanding. Thus, once we understand what a whole is and what a part is, we immediately understand that it is true to say that a whole is greater than any of its parts; once we understand what being is, we know immediately that being is not non-being; once we know what is meant by the same and other we understand that the same cannot simultaneously be the other.

Among the truths of understanding recognized by human beings once they know what the realities are that are related to one another in propositions is the truth that a genuine human good ought to be pursued and that evil ought to be avoided. And, as we have just seen, it is possible for human beings to discover, through reflection on their experiences, that certain realities correspond to needs that they have as human beings and that these realities are genuinely good for human beings: e.g., life, health, justice, friendship, knowledge, peace, etc. Man needs these goods—they make him more human—because the being that he is requires these goods for its own completion. The task of moral thinking, subsequently, is to determine just how these goods are to be pursued and how they can be destroyed in and through human actions.

The relativistic stance taken by Hume, Ayer, and others makes a great deal of the difference between "is" and "ought" and much has been written on this issue during the past fifty years. But it is important to note that "is" thinking differs from "ought" thinking or "is to be" thinking. "Is" thinking, that is, the kind of thinking reflected in the analytical and factual judgments alone deemed worthy of being called true or false by people like Ayer, is concerned with knowing reality as it actually is. It is not knowledge that is ordered *directly* to action, although it can be. But "is to be" thinking, of which "ought" thinking is a special mode, is quite different, for it *is* directly ordered to what we are to do, to what "is to be" through our activity. And it is precisely this kind of thinking that is governed by the basic human goods or values that function, as consciously known and articulated, as principles or intelligent behavior, principles of practical reason, guides to choosing.

Finally, in order to bring to completion this section of our investigation into the way we come to know the human, it should be noted that a purely relativistic position eviscerates our human deeds of their intelligibility.

As McCabe has noted, our actions not only get something done; they get something said. They play a role in human communication. This means that they have something to say about our identity as human or moral beings. On the relativistic theory, their rightness or wrongness (their human significance) is not something that they possess because of what they are but is something that accrues to them as a result of the feelings or opinions or judgments of various groups or individuals. The point is not that these acts are valuable "in themselves," for there is no such thing as an action in itself. Rather it is that human acts, human deeds, emerge from human beings, relate human beings to one another, and play a role in the communication between and among men. Because they do this, they are realities that possess discernible features; they are intelligible and meaningful, and it is possible for human beings to discover their meaning.

II

"Getting to know the human" is a subject that has many dimensions. In the preceding section our interest was focused on the intelligibility of human deeds, practices, and institutions and the issue of ethical relativity. Here I want to center attention on the *social* character of the process whereby we grow into our knowledge of the human, a subject that obviously has close connection to the themes that have just been considered and one that helps to illumine these themes and, indeed, the meaning of human existence as a co-existence, of man as a being who is a being with.

When we are born (and in fact during that period of our lives when we are still unborn yet living in our mother's womb) we are certainly human beings. But in order for us to grow into the human in all its dimensions, including knowledge of the "human" or "right" or "good," we must go through a process that is variously called humanization, socialization, or simply human growth and development. We are initiated, as it were, into the human community and quite specifically we are initiated into a *particular* human community, one that has already been in existence and has had time to reflect on human experiences and offer interpretations of these experiences, including the moral experiences of the persons belonging to the community. In order for us to become initiated into the particular human community, to "find" or discover ourselves within it, and to be able to communicate with the other human beings who are members of this community, we must learn the language of this community, and this "language" is not only the tongue or speech common to its members but its "way of life" and its way of perceiving and understanding the world. In short, in the process of humanization or of growing into the human, the "world" we enter is a world that is, in the words of Bernard Lonergan, "mediated to us by meaning."[21] We cannot "become" human or grow into the human unless we become familiar with the world in which we exist, and this world is a world whose meaning is immediately constituted for us by the communities in which we live.

The point that Lonergan, as a philosopher-theologian, attempts to make when he speaks of our entering a world that is mediated to us by meaning parallels or is even identical with, I believe, the point that sociologists such as Peter Berger and Thomas Luckmann are trying to make when they attempt to describe the process of socialization. According to these writers the process of becoming a member of a society is required inasmuch as individual human beings, who are by reason of their character as animals of a particular species *predisposed to* sociality, actually become members of a society or community by entering into that society and developing the capability to live humanly within it.[22] For Berger and Luckmann this process occurs on two levels. The first level, which they term "primary socialization," introduces the individual into all of the essential institutions of the society, whereas "secondary socialization" communicates the more particular or specialized knowledge that individual human beings will need to fulfill their own specific roles within that society.[23] Their major point is set forth as follows:

Man is biologically predestined to construct and inhabit a world with others. This world becomes for him the dominant and definitive reality. Its limits are set by nature, but once constructed this world acts back on nature. In the dialectic between nature and the socially constructed world the human organism itself is transformed. In this same dialectic man produces reality and thereby produces himself.[24]

Berger and Luckmann and other sociologists speak of "the social construction of reality," and I believe that what they have in mind when they speak in this way is precisely what Lonergan has in mind when he speaks of a "world mediated to us by meaning." It is this world, moreover, that comprises the *human reality* that we encounter in the process of humanization or socialization. It is not brute facticity, sheer empirical data, but a reality that is already suffused with meaning, and part of the meaning that this reality has is concerned with the human good and with the "values" and "goods" that go to make up the *bonum humanum* in its plenitude.

This "world mediated by meaning" or this "socially constructed reality" is the real, living human world into which each of us is initiated. This world can, as Berger and Luckmann among others indicate, become "reified," that is, made into an objective "thing" or brute fact that is simply *there* and must be accepted as it is;[25] unfortunately, this is all too frequently the case. But this humanly structured reality can also be creatively modified by human beings themselves. This, at any rate, is the way the Berger-Luckmann sociological analysis understands the situation. Their understanding, I believe—and it is important to note that their understanding is rooted in empirical studies of the dynamics of human societies—parallels the philosophical analysis that Lonergan gives of the spontaneous movement of the inquiring animal we call man from experiencing to understanding to a true understanding to responsible action.[26] For Lonergan the human world into which we are initiated is a meaningful world—it is a world where the experiences that men have had have been understood to have specifiable meanings. But, and this is the important element, the meanings that the human beings have discovered in experience and that have been formally articulated and given institutional expression in the very particular communities in which we live, are capable of being questioned in the light of new experiences. The *truth* of these meanings can be called into question and the quest for verifying or falsifying these meanings is an on-going yet *directed* process. It is an on-going quest because the final, definitive answer to the questioning behind our drive to know the human cannot be given, simply because the human in its normative sense is so inexhaustibly rich in meaning. But it is directed because negatively we can, through critical reflection on experience and on the meanings given to experience, come to see that certain kinds of deeds, practices, and institutions are simply inhuman. These deeds, practices, institutions may have made sense at one stage in the course of man's development—for anything that a human being does as a purposeful being is ordered to some basic human good, as we have already seen—but they are now seen as being distorted, far too partial expressions of what it means to be a human being.

Perhaps some examples may clarify what I mean here. Take the case of the institution of slavery in human societies. Slavery served some basic human needs and fostered some basic human goods—the life and health and well-being of the societies that accepted slavery. Yet it is obvious that the institution of slavery, although it served the needs of *some* men and aided *them* in their struggle to achieve the real goods that go to make up the human good, *destroyed* these same goods in the slaves. Because slavery did serve some human needs and procure some human goods and because the institution of slavery was an element of the "human world" of meaning into which persons born into societies practicing slavery were initiated, it could be and was perceived by those initiated into that society as something "valuable," as something "good." It could be reified into a factual condition that simply had to be accepted just because it was there. But the lived experiences of people within such societies, including the slaves themselves, clamored for attention, demanded an answer; and gradually the consciousness that this institution did indeed destroy basic human goods, goods intended for all men simply because they are men, could raise new questions to challenge the truthfulness of the claim that slavery is a good, a value. Because man is the inquiring, questioning animal driven to understand his experiences and to reach a true understanding of his experiences, progress is possible. Reality-making or truth-making factors that were perhaps hidden or dimly perceived within a society can be discovered because of new experiences and new questions about experience.

This is the way, it can be suggested, that men and cultures and communities "grow" into the human. It is a way that seems supported by the sociological analyses of men like Berger and Luckmann and by the philosophical analysis of writers like Lonergan. And it is a way that explains the fact of wide cultural diversity without leading to ethical relativity. For on this view the differences in values or appraisals of the good that we find among differing cultures and individuals is explained in terms of the differing experiences and understandings of experiences that cultures have in their struggle to secure the real goods of men. On this view what is valuable or good is so not because it is *thought* to be or *opined* to be so but because of reality-making or truth-making factors. The thinking and opinions whereby human experiences are given meaning and thus structured into a reality of human significance for those being initiated into specific human communities do not make a value to be a value or a good to be a good. Rather the thinking and opinions are truthful to the extent that they are predicated on the real relations among men that do indeed provide us with truth-making or reality-making factors.

Notes

1. John Dewey, *Human Nature and Conduct* (New York: Modern Library, 1930), p. 92.

2. Ruth Benedict, *Patterns of Culture* (Boston: Houghton Mifflin, 1961), pp. 233-240.

3. Montaigne, *Essays*, Bk. I, no. 40.

4. See Hume's *A Treatise on Human Nature,* Selby-Bigge ed., pp. 308-309, and the introduction to his *An Inquiry Concerning Human Understanding.*

5. A. J. Ayer, *Language, Truth and Logic* (New York: Dover, 1956), pp. 107-108.

6. This, I believe, is the root reason why various consequentialist approaches to determining the rightness or wrongness of human acts are erroneous. This will be seen more clearly subsequently, in the chapter on human acts, but the point I am trying to make might be seen if we note an instructive comment by Joseph Fletcher, whose position is basically consequentialist, in his *Situation Ethics* (Philadelphia: Westminster, 1965), p. 77: "Cicero, in his *De legibus*, I. 17, 45, said seriously, 'Only a madman could maintain that the distinction between the honorable and the dishonorable, between virtue and vice, is a matter of opinion, not of nature.' This is nevertheless precisely and exactly what situation ethics maintains." In other words, a human deed, practice, or institution is honorable not by reason of anything really present in and discernible in the deed, practice, or institution but simply by reason of the way the deed, practice, or institution is evaluated —and for Fletcher it is ultimately evaluated good by its consequences.

7. Richard B. Brandt, "Ethical Relativism" in *The Encyclopedia of Philosophy* edited by Paul Edwards (New York: Macmillan and Free Press, 1967), III, 75.

8. Henry Veatch, *Rational Man* (Bloomington, Ind.: University of Indiana Press, 1962), p. 45.

9. Lawrence Kohlberg, "Stages of Moral Development as a Basis for Moral Education," in *Moral Education: Interdisciplinary Approaches,* edited by C. M. Beck, B. S. Crittenden, and E. V. Sullivan (New York: Newman, 1971), p. 39 ff.

10. *Ibid.,* pp. 32-41.

11. Herbert McCabe, *What Is Ethics All About?* (Washington: Corpus, 1968), pp. 44-45.

12. Ernest Hilgard, *Introduction to Psychology* (New York: Harcourt, 1962), pp. 124-144.

13. Robert Lowie, *Introduction to Cultural Anthropology* (New York: Rinehart, 1940). Grisez discusses the views of Hilgard and Lowie in his *Contraception and the Natural Law* (Milwaukee: The Bruce Publishing Company, 1964), pp. 60-72, where he develops his position regarding basic human goods as principles of practical reason. See also Grisez, *Abortion: The Myths, the Realities, and the Arguments* (New York: Corpus, 1970), pp. 307-321.

14. On Lonergan, see above, Chapter One, pp. 3-4, 6 and note 5.

15. Grisez, *Abortion. . . .* p. 313. See also the recent work Grisez coauthored with Russell Shaw, *Beyond the New Morality: The Responsibilities of Freedom* (Notre Dame, Ind.: University of Notre Dame Press, 1974), especially Chapters Seven and Eight.

16. *Ibid.*, p. 314.

17. *Ibid.*, p. 314ff.

18. Kohlberg, *art. cit.*, p. 58.

19. Mortimer Adler, *The Time of Our Lives* (New York: Holt, Rinehart, and Winston, 1971), p. 124 ff.

20. *Ibid.*, p. 137 ff.

21. On this entire subject see Bernard J. F. Lonergan, *Insight* (New York: Philosophical Library, 1957), chapter 17. See also David Tracy, *The Achievement of Bernard Lonergan* (New York: Herder & Herder, 1971), pp. 47-55.

22. Peter Berger and Thomas Luckmann, *The Social Construction of Reality: A Treatise in the Sociology of Knowledge* (New York: Doubleday, 1966), p. 119.

23. *Ibid.*, pp. 120-136.

24. *Ibid.*, p. 168.

25. *Ibid.*, p. 82. It would, incidentally, be useful to compare the way Herbert McCabe (*op. cit.*) describes the process whereby men enter into *linguistic* unity or form linguistic communities in which it is possible to share and communicate life with the Berger-Luckmann description of the process of socialization.

26. See Lonergan, *Method in Theology* (New York: Herder & Herder, 1972), p. 16 ff.

Chapter Three:

GROWING INTO THE HUMAN CONSCIENTIOUSLY

Becoming human is evidently a process, a development, a growth. It is a process that each of us undergoes or, better, in which we actively participate. And we participate in this process both as individuals and as members of the various communities in which we discover our identity, in which we struggle to find ourselves. One of the elements that play a role in our growth into the human is what we call conscience. How often have we not heard it said that we ought to "follow our conscience," to "act conscientiously," to "let conscience be our guide." But what is it that we are talking about when we speak of conscience? To some it is a still small voice, a kind of moral monitor urging us to do this and avoid that. Others regard it as a special and innate human faculty providing us with the ability to grasp intuitively right and wrong. Still others look upon it as the superego described in the following terms by Sigmund Freud:

> The long period of childhood during which the
> growing human being lives in dependence on
> his parents leaves behind it a precipitate,
> which forms within his ego a special agency
> in which this parental influence is prolonged.
> It has received the name of "superego." The
> parents' influence naturally includes not only
> the personalities of the parents themselves
> but also the racial, national and family tradi-
> tions handed on through them, as well as the
> demands of the immediate social milieu
> which they represent.[1]

Surely the agency designated by the Freudian superego influences human behavior and the process of our growth into the human. It certainly has a part to play in the "social construction of reality" of which Peter Berger and Thomas Luckmann write or in what Bernard Lonergan terms the mediation to us of a humanly meaningful world. Yet to identify what moralists mean by conscience with the superego would be a mistake. Some simple considerations will help to show why.

Frequently during the course of our lives we find it necessary to oppose, and to oppose vigorously and, at times, at great suffering or inconvenience to ourselves, practices and attitudes "demanded" by our "immediate social milieu." For example, our parents and "the racial, national and family traditions handed on through them" may regard social relationships and friendship with members of another racial or ethnic group as unacceptable, wrong, something to be avoided. They may consider it wrong for women to become involved in political and social activity, or they may think it perfectly permissible to bar people from certain jobs if they entertain specific kinds of ideas. Because of the influence of the superego we are inclined to endorse these attitudes and to act in accordance with them. Nonetheless, because of our own experiences and our own attempts to discover the true meaning of these experiences we sometimes find it necessary to reject, and to reject *in the name of conscience,* attitudes and practices bearing the superego's stamp of approval. Because of this Robert White is surely correct when he writes.:

We shall regard this superego as a childhood conscience . . . borrowed straight from parental sanctions *without reflection or the use of his own experience on the part of the child.* Mature conscience begins when the child's sympathy and insight get to work so that he sees a purpose—other than pleasing his parents—behind restraints and ideals. It continues when he discriminates the effects of his actions on everyone who is affected by them, judging his acts accordingly and freeing himself from blind literal obedience . . .[2]

Perhaps it could be suggested that the superego exerts its major influence on human conduct during the first three stages in the development of an individual's moral being as described by Lawrence Kohlberg. During the first two stages, which comprise what Kohlberg calls the "preconventional level" of moral development, "the child is responsive to cultural rules and labels of good and bad, right or wrong, but interprets these labels in terms of either the physical or the hedonistic consequences of action . . . or in

55

terms of the physical power of those who enunciate the rules and labels."[3] During the third or "good boy—nice girl" stage, which initiates what Kohlberg calls the "conventional level" of moral growth, "good behaviour is that which pleases or helps others and is approved by them."[4] It is obvious that during these stages of a person's growth into the human behavior is not so much self-controlled as it is governed by forces external to the person himself.

Many psychoanalysts, among them Gregory Zilboorg, have written perceptively of the differences between an authentic moral conscience and the Freudian superego.[5] A very helpful schema noting the contrasting characteristics that exist between the superego and genuine conscience has been prepared by John Glaser in an informative and illuminating article on the topic, and it will be worthwhile to offer his conclusions here. From his study of the pertinent literature reflecting on man's moral experience Glaser contrasts superego and conscience as follows:

SUPEREGO	CONSCIENCE
commands that an act be performed for approval, in order to make oneself lovable, accepted; fear of love-withdrawal is the basis	invites to action, to love, and in this very act of other-directed commitment to cocreate self-value
introverted: the thematic center is a sense of one's own value	extroverted: the thematic center is the value which invites; self-value is concomitant and secondary to this

static: does not grow, does not learn; cannot function creatively in a new situation; merely repeats a basic command

dynamic: an awareness and sensitivity to value which develops and grows; a mind-set which can precisely function in a new situation

authority-figure-oriented: not a question of perceiving and responding to a value but of "obeying" authority's command "blindly"

value-oriented: the value or disvalue is perceived and responded to, regardless of whether authority has commanded or not

"atomized" units of activity are its object

individual acts are seen in their importance as a part of a larger process or pattern

past-oriented: primarily concerned with cleaning up the record with regard to past acts

future-oriented: creative; sees the past as having a future and helping to structure this future as a better future

urge to be punished and thereby earn reconciliation

sees the need to repair by structuring the future orientation toward the value in question (which includes making good past harms)

rapid transition from severe isolation, guilt feelings, etc. to a sense of self-value accomplished by confessing to an authority figure

a sense of the gradual process of growth which characterizes all dimensions of genuine personal development

possible great disproportion between guilt experienced and the value in question; extent of guilt depends more on weight of authority figure and "volume" with which he speaks rather than density of the value in question[6]

experience of guilt proportionate to the importance of the value in question, even though authority may never have addressed this specific value

From the preceding considerations we can see that the reality of moral conscience is quite different from Freud's superego. But what exactly is conscience? To answer this question it will be helpful, I believe, to note first some perceptive comments by John Macquarrie, the noted Scottish theologian whose ecumenical spirit and deep love of the Christian theological tradition are joined with a genuine understanding and appreciation of contemporary philosophical thought. Macquarrie, after noting the ambiguity that surrounds the term *conscience,* observes that it is possible to distinguish several levels of conscience. At one level the term *conscience* is used to designate the struggle that goes on when we are faced with some particular occasion of choice and are attempting to decide on the "right" or "human" course of action. In this sense conscience is what older writers, preeminently St. Thomas Aquinas, had in mind when they spoke of conscience as an *act* of judging, as the final judgment of "practical reason" or of our intelligence as ordered to action. In this sense conscience refers to a termination of a process of thought with respect to a particular moral situation. It is our own personal judgment that this specific course of action is right and ought to be done or that it is wrong and that we have an obligation not to do it.[7]

At another level, Macquarrie writes, conscience can mean "a broader . . . more generalized knowledge of right and wrong, of good and bad."[8] At this level conscience corresponds to what older moralists called the habit of synderesis or synteresis.[9] This was conceived as the habit of first moral principles that could serve as the basic premises from which moral reasoning could begin. The principles of synderesis were considered as basic starting points on which one could base true judgments about the rightness and wrongness—the humanness or inhumanness—of human acts. In brief, synderesis refers to what we can legitimately call "principles of intelligent activity" or what the Scholastics called "principles of practical reason." These principles, as we have already seen,[10] are discovered by us as we reflect on our experiences to discern their human meaning. These principles serve, as we have noted in our discussion of the views of Lawrence Kohlberg and Germain Grisez, as the general guides to choice. They are intelligent principles rooted in the real goods corresponding to real needs that we have simply because we are human beings. These principles do not specify precise kinds of acts that we must do or not do if we are to become human, but they do sketch out the broad categories or genera of actions that are choiceworthy. Among such principles we could include the following: Be just, respect life, honor truth.[11]

The third level of conscience to which Macquarrie refers is "a special and very fundamental mode of self-awareness—the awareness of 'how it is with oneself.' "[12] At this level conscience is indeed, as the Fathers of Vatican II put it, "the most secret core and sanctuary of a man."[13] The character of conscience as a special mode of self-awareness is indicated in the etymology of the word. Our English term derives from the Latin *conscientia*, a term that means both *consciousness* and *conscience*. As a special mode of self-awareness conscience has as its basic function the disclosure of ourselves to ourselves. As Macquarrie puts it:

Specifically, conscience discloses the gap between our actual selves and that image of ourselves that we have already in virtue of the "natural inclination" toward the fulfillment of man's end. Thus conscience is not merely a disclosure; it is also, as Heidegger insists, a call or summons. It is a call to that full humanity of which we already have some idea or image because of the very fact that we are human at all, and that our nature is to exist, to go out beyond where we are at any given moment. Although we commonly think of conscience as commanding us to *do* certain things, the fundamental command of conscience is to *be*.[14]

One element of our experience as human beings that compels our reflection is the fact that we can, and frequently do, accuse ourselves from the depths of our being because we *know* that through our deeds we have, in truth, done wrong and that we have done so knowingly. We realize that we have taken on, as part of our personal identity, the identity of an evil-doer. I am not speaking here of the false sense of shame or guilt that we sometimes experience. This, I believe, can be linked to the Freudian superego; it is an indication of immaturity. Rather I am referring to an authentic sense of guilt, of remorse. And this is a real component of human experience. The very fact that we can distinguish between neurotic or false guilt and genuine guilt requires an explanation.[15] If we are able to make judgments of this kind about ourselves, there must be within us the conditions making judgments of this kind possible. This means that there is, present to the depths of our being, some image or self-understanding that we realize we are violating or have violated.

Earlier, in discussing the Freudian superego, we mentioned that it seems to play a dominant role in our lives during the early stages of moral growth or development, when our behavior is not so much self-controlled as it is subject to forces outside our own control. Perhaps by reflecting on the concept of *control* we can see more clearly what Macquarrie has in mind when he speaks of a level of conscience that refers to a special mode of self-awareness. The English word *control* derives from the French *contrôler,* which in turn stems from the Latin *contra* (against) and *rotulus* (a roll). In its original English meaning the term thus meant "to check or verify payments or what have you by comparing them with a duplicate register." It thus acquired the meaning of regulating or governing or of exercising authority, with the implication that this entailed the use of restraints in order to curb tendencies or forces opposed to authority. With this understanding of *control* as a background, let us now reflect on the relationship between conscience and the control or regulation of our deeds, of our behavior or conduct.

Behavior is controlled when it is regulated by some authority, when it corresponds to some "register" or "norm"; whereas behavior is *un*controlled when it is unrestrained by any authority and fails to correspond to a "register" or "norm." Behavior, moreover, does not exist in itself; behavior implies an activity, a doing, and implies that this doing has a doer, that it emerges from a being who is its "author." When we speak of *human* behavior, the doer in question is obviously man. Human behavior, thus, is controlled if it corresponds to what we could call a human norm or register, and is uncontrolled when it is not faithful to this norm. And here we are faced with the question that has confronted us from the beginning: What is the normative human? It can be suggested that normative human behavior is behavior that is fitting for a being who can be called human. Now a human being is, as we have already seen, an intelligent, inquiring, questioning being capable of speaking and

61

communicating with his fellows. Human existence, moreover, as we have seen, is a coexistence, and the search of each human being for his own identity, his own destiny, is a search he shares in common with all men. It is a meaningful and not an absurd search because there really are some goods that correspond to needs rooted in man because he is the kind of being he is and because these goods really do make each man more human.

These various goods that go to make human beings more human (life, health, friendship, justice, peace, etc.) are obviously related to our activities, to our behavior. Because we are intelligent beings who can ask questions and communicate with other men, we can know that we are doers and we can know what the acts we do *mean*. We can, in short, be consciously aware that our acts (our behavior) not only bring about certain kinds of results but also play a role in our communication with others and in our search for identity and meaning in our lives. We can understand that our behavior has something to say, something to tell us about what it means to be a human being.

With this perspective, I think that we can appreciate what Macquarrie is attempting to say when he speaks about the level of conscience as a deep-seated self-awareness. For he is telling us something that is central to the view of man in the Judeo-Christian tradition and in Western civilization, namely, that men are capable of *self*-control. And we are capable of self-control because the "norm" or "register" against which our behavior is to be checked is *within* us; it is rooted in our intelligence whereby we are able to question experience, interpret it or discover its meaning, test its meaning for truth, and act responsibly in accordance with our true understanding of our experience. Because we are beings who are consciously present to ourselves, that is, aware of ourselves as intelligent and inquiring beings, we are *conscientious* beings, capable of exercising *self*-control and of regulating or governing our behavior according to a norm or "register" that is immanent to ourselves, namely our being as moral beings, our "nature."

Obviously our character as self-conscious, conscientious beings is linked to our existence as freely responsible beings, as genuine moral agents, and this is a theme that must be taken up explicitly later on.[16] At present we shall accept human freedom, in the sense of our freedom to determine our own lives and control our own activities, as an assumption implicit in our awareness of ourselves as conscious, conscientious beings.

There is obviously a relationship between the various levels of conscience of which Macquarrie speaks; and if we reflect upon the connection between conscience as the termination of a process of thought, that is, as the judgment *here and now* that we ought to do this or ought not to do that, and conscience as a special mode of self-awareness, we will see why we are obliged to "follow our conscience" in the sense that we are obliged to act in accordance with our own best judgment about the rightness or wrongness of a specific course of action. The function of conscience as a basic form of self-awareness or self-consciousness is to disclose us to ourselves and to summon us to become more fully human to become what we are meant to be. But to become what we are meant to be, to become more fully human, we are to do good and avoid evil. The judgment that we make, conscientiously, that *this* act here and now is the good that I am obliged to do or the evil that I must avoid if I am to be faithful to the "me" that I am in virtue of my being human at all, is our own personal way of knowing what we must do if we are to answer the call or summons to become what we are meant to be. Consequently, to act in a way that contradicts our own best judgment means that we are willing, in the depths of our being, to "intend and effect evil." It means that we are willing to violate the image of ourselves that we have deep within ourselves in virtue of the fact that we are human beings, that is, beings with a vocation. It means that we are willing to violate our own selves, to deny our own humanity. It means that we are *un*willing to respond to the situation before us in the way that we ourselves have judged to be the fitting response that ought to be made to that situation by one who calls himself a human being.

The obligation to "follow our conscience" in the sense of our own best judgment about the rightness or wrongness of a specific course of action assumes, of course, that in making this judgment we are being responsive to the truth, to the reality-making factors of the situation, and that we are not hiding our heads in the sand or closing our eyes and minds to the truth. It assumes, in other words, that in reaching our conscientious judgment we are being conscientious or true to ourselves and to reality.

It is clear that the judgment we make in any specific instance may be erroneous. But even if the judgment is erroneous, we are still obliged to act in accord with it, because for us, at the time the judgment is made, this judgment *is* the true judgment. We do not, in other words, realize that it is erroneous. We are not conscious that it is false. The error in our judgment is an error not of our own making; it is not a willed error and thus its erroneousness has not been ratified or endorsed by us as persons.[17] It is true *for* us in the sense that it is only by acting in accord with our own best judgment (conscience in *this* sense) that we can be faithful to ourselves as conscious, conscientious beings (conscience in the sense of a deep-seated self-awareness).

Here it is necessary to stress that we do have the obligation, in making judgments about the rightness or wrongness of possible courses of action, to be conscientious in making the judgments. This is implied in the meaning of the term itself. As we have already noted, *conscience* derives etymologically from the Latin *con-scientia*. This means that conscience is literally a "with knowledge," or, as Albert Jonsen has suggested in a recent book, a "knowing with."[18] In our struggle to know we depend on others, because our existence, as we have noted so frequently, is a *co*-existence, and being human is being *with* others. We live in a world with and for our fellowmen, and our fellowmen and our life with them provide us with the supportive context we need in our attempt to reflect on experience in order to discover its true meaning and to act responsibly in accordance with the truth. It is only reasonable, then, to consider the reasoned judgments of others in the process of thinking that we undertake in our own personal effort to reach a true judgment about a moral situation. In other words, because we live in a world that is mediated to us by meaning, in a world whose "reality" is in part the result of a social construction, we cannot ignore this fact if we are to be conscientious in making our own judgments about the rightness or wrongness of proposed courses of action.

For Roman Catholics the obligation to be conscientious in making judgments about moral situations includes the obligation to be open to and responsive to the teachings of the Church as these are expressed by the magisterium, that is, by the Pope and the bishops in communion with him. And this obligation raises the serious question of possible conflict between one's own personal conscience and authority. According to the Fathers of Vatican II (and to the entire tradition of Catholic Christianity) the Pope and the entire body of bishops in union with him have particular responsibility and competence with respect to matters of faith and morals. In the *Constitution on the Church,* for example, we read:

Bishops, teaching in communion with the Roman Pontiff, are to be respected by all as witnesses to divine and Catholic truth. In matters of faith and morals, the bishops speak in the name of Christ and the faithful are to accept their teaching and adhere to it with a religious assent of soul. This religious submission of will and of mind must be shown in a special way to the authentic teaching authority of the Roman Pontiff, even when he is not speaking ex cathedra. That is, it must be shown in such a way that his supreme magisterium is acknowledged with reverence, the judgments made by him are sincerely adhered to, according to his manifest mind and will.[19]

Does this mean that it is impossible for a faithful Catholic to dissent from any teaching of the magisterium? What happens if a Catholic, after conscientiously seeking to make the best judgment about a given activity, judges in a way that contradicts the judgment of the magisterium? Is he then required to act against his own judgment, his own conscience, and in accord with the judgment of the magisterium? Or is he still obliged to act in accord with his own final judgment about the matter?

To answer these questions we ought first to note that the same council that stressed the "religious assent of soul" that the faithful owe to the teachings of the magisterium, even if they are not manifestly infallible, also insisted that a human being's conscience is his innermost core and sanctuary, where he "is alone with God, whose voice echoes in his depths."[20] If we couple this teaching of Vatican II with the theological tradition rooted in the thought of St. Thomas[21] that one not only is free to follow a conscience that is erroneous but is indeed obliged to do so if the error is not attributable to an unwillingness to seek the truth, we can conclude that a human being has a moral obligation to act according to his own conscientious judgment, even if this judgment does in fact differ from that of the teaching Church. While acknowledging this, however, we must not lose sight of the fact that a Catholic, in developing his own conscientious judgments, can do so conscientiously only if he is willing to listen to the teaching of the Church and take pains to make it his own unless he cannot do so without violating that self-awareness that he has in virtue of being human.

Because this is such a troubling question the comments of Richard A. McCormick, S. J., may prove helpful. In an article in which he surveyed thelogical literature on this vexing problem in the wake of the debates at Vatican II on religious liberty and within the Catholic community over the question of contraception, McCormick found it necessary to speak directly to the agonizing dilemma posed by the Council's declaration (previously cited) that a "religious assent of soul" must be given to the authentic but noninfallible teachings of the magisterium. Putting this declaration within the framework of the ecclesiology provided by the Council as a whole, McCormick wrote as follows:

The Second Vatican Council enlarged our notion of the Church by moving away somewhat from the juridical model. The dominant description of the Church became the People of God. If this notion of the Church is weighed carefully, would it not affect the notion of the Church as teacher? Just one of the effects would be a clearer separation of teaching and administration. In light of this separation, magisterial teachings would not be viewed as "imposed, commanded, demanding submission and obedience"; for these terms suggest disciplinary jurisdiction, not teaching authority. Rather, noninfallible Church teachings would be seen as offered to the faithful. Obviously, such teaching must still be viewed as authoritative, but the term "authoritative" would shed many of its juridical, and sometimes almost military, connotations. The proportionate response to authoritative teaching might not *immediately* be religious assent, even though such acceptance would generally follow. Perhaps the matter could be put as follows. Because of its indisputable charism . . . the hierarchical magisterium must be accepted as an authoritative teacher. That is, for a Catholic the teachings of the magisterium enjoy an eminence not conceded to any other religious teacher. This means that its teachings will generate a presumption not enjoyed by other teaching authorities. . . . It would seem that the *immediate* response to such a presumption in a concrete case is not assent, but rather more generally a religious docility and deference . . . a kind of connatural eagerness to accept and adhere to this teaching. . . . This strong inclination would concretize itself in several ways. First, it will mean respect and reverence for the person and his office, and continuing openness to his teaching. Secondly, it will mean a readiness to reassess one's own positions in light of this teaching, an attempt to see if this teaching can be supported on grounds other than those presented, and a humble realization of the limitations imposed by one's own background, etc. Thirdly, it will suggest a great reluctance to conclude that magisterial moral teaching is clearly erroneous even after one has concluded that the evidence, arguments, and analyses used to establish this teaching are inadequate. . . . Finally, it will demand a style of external behavior which fosters respect and support for the magisterium.[22]

The type of response to authentic yet noninfallible teachings of the magisterium on moral questions suggested by McCormick seems, at least initially, to be both realistic and reasonable. It recognizes the moral imperative that requires each human person to exercise responsibility over his own judgments and choices and to decide on the basis of his own best judgment, his conscientious judgment, and at the same time it acknowledges the duty that a Catholic has to take seriously the teachings of the magisterium in making his conscientious judgments—and this latter duty, it should be noted, is in reality a more specific instance of the obligation that every human being has to listen to others, to his fellowmen with whom and for whom he lives, in his struggle to grow into the human.

Although I believe that McCormick's approach to this issue is basically sound and is not intended to minimize the teaching authority of the magisterium on moral questions, his way of characterizing noninfallible yet authentic teachings of the magisterium on moral issues is somewhat weak. These teachings are not simply "offered to the faithful" in the way that a moral theologian such as McCormick himself or Curran might offer a judgment on a moral issue to the Christian people. That is, they do not constitute what one could call simply one more theological "opinion" about the humanness of a given activity or practice. Rather, they represent the "mind the Church," the considered judgment of the Church about the moral significance of an activity or practice. Thus, it would follow that only the most compelling and serious reasons would warrant rightful dissent from a noninfallible yet authentic teaching of the magisterium.

One final comment concerning conflicting judgments of individuals and the teaching Church (or, more broadly, any kind of public authority) seems necessary here. Any proposed course of action is right or wrong, human or inhuman, *not* because it is declared to be so by the teaching Church or any teaching authority, but because of reality-making or truth-making factors. If the Church teaches that something is wrong, it is not wrong because the Church teaches that it is; rather the Church teaches that it is wrong because it really is wrong. Because of a Catholic's belief that Jesus abides in his Church and has sent to his Church the Spirit of truth, he can confidently expect that the Church will be speaking truthfully in making judgments about moral issues; but it is possible that in some specific instance the judgment of the Church's teaching authority may be erroneous, and it is this possibility, combined with the obligation of every human being, as he grows into the human, to make his own responsible judgments in determining his own life, that provides the basis for legitimate dissent. Just as the declaration or judgment of the Church or any teaching authority does not *make* something be right or human, so too the conscientious judgment of a human being does not do this. In the next chapter we shall seek to specify the reality-making or truth-making factors that do indeed determine the rightness and wrongness of our deeds. Our concern here has been to see why a human being is obliged to act in accord with his own conscientious judgment, and how this obligation reveals the relationship between conscience as an act of judging terminating a process of thought and conscience as a deep-seated self-awareness.

From what has been said thus far, the meaning of the injunction to "follow one's conscience" ought to be clear, and it ought also to be clear *why* this obligation exists. From personal experience, however, we know that we do not always follow our own conscientious judgment, that we do not always do what we ourselves have judged to be the right thing for us to do if we are to answer the summons to become the kind of beings we are meant to be. How is this possible? It seems almost absurd that we would go ahead and act in a way that we have personally judged to be destructive of our own moral being. Yet that we can and do act in this way is one of the most poignant experiences that human beings have, an experience indicative of the mystery of human existence, of the meaning of man as a moral being.

Although we can and do act directly against our own conscientious judgments it would seem for the most part, as Macquarrie points out,[23] that we do not *directly* act against our own best judgment. Rather we try to refigure the situation in order to "select out" or "select in" features that will support a different judgment. But in doing this we realize that we are really kidding ourselves, that we are engaged in a process of self-deception, that we are not "conscientiously" reaching a judgment of conscience. Why do we do this? Perhaps no final answer can be given to this question; but the reason may lie, at least in part, in the fact that our loves, our desires, are not properly ordered to the *bonum humanum,* to the full range of the real goods that together go up to make human beings more human. Our loves and desires are fixed on these goods as goods *for us,* not as goods *of* all men. What this shows is that man's moral life is not simply a matter of knowing. There is the mystery of human freedom whereby we can seek to flee from ourselves, from our own humanity, and pretend that we are rightfully pursuing a true good in a human way when we know in our hearts, in the depths of our being, that our pursuit is either for a good that is only apparent or is a wrongful pursuit of a true good, and when we really know that our pursuit is one that will destroy our moral being and alienate us from ourselves.

There is thus a difference between the judgment of conscience, understood as the termination of a process of thinking whereby we judge that we ought here and now do this or not do that, and the choice itself that we actually make. This difference leads us to consider, at least briefly, what older philosophers and theologians called the virtue of prudence. By prudence here is not meant the shrewd calculating that will best serve the ease and comfort of the individual. Quite to the contrary, for by prudence here is meant both a clearsighted vision of the truth and a willingness to act in accordance with the truth. The prudent man of Aristotle and Aquinas is the one who is ready to follow the transcendental imperatives of which Lonergan speaks;[24] he is the person whose mind is open to truth and reality, whose will is ready to give to others what is rightfully theirs, whose passions and emotions are under his control, not he under theirs. He is the man who has the courage to do what he knows to be right even if in doing so he may disturb the status quo, risk inconvenience to himself, imperil himself. The prudent man of older philosophers and theologians is not discussed much in contemporary moral literature, nor has much been written recently about the virtue of prudence. But contemporary writers have developed an analogous notion, namely that of responsibility and the responsible person. Responsibility is a key theme in contemporary religious ethics,[25] and the parallels between the responsible person in the ethics of writers like Bonhoeffer, Häring, Richard Niebuhr and others and the prudent man of Aquinas and his modern disciple Josef Pieper are remarkable. The prudent or responsible man is the person who is responsive to the lives of other people. He is the man who responds to reality, who is open to truth and to being. The prudent man, as described by Thomas Aquinas and Pieper, is the man whose reason has been made perfect by knowledge of the truth and who inwardly shapes his desires and choices by his knowledge of the truth.[26] The prudent man, in other words, is the person who will form his conscience responsibly, conscientiously, and who will *choose to act* in conformity to his own informed judgments.

Yet conscience, in the sense of consciousness or deep-seated self-awareness, discloses that our moral life is much more complex than an idealistic sketch of the prudent or responsible man may indicate. In saying this, I in no way wish to deny or reject what has just been said about prudence and responsibility; I merely want to make it clear that our moral lives as conscious and conscientious beings are teeming with life and have depths immensely difficult to probe. I also wish to counter an individualistic ethic that would see our progress in the human as a matter of "pulling ourselves up by our own bootstraps," as it were. What I have in mind can best be understood, I think, by citing again the passage from St. Paul in which he writes: "I do not understand my own actions. . . . For I do not do what I want, but the evil I do not want is what I do" (Romans 7:15-19). These words of Paul are a useful reminder that we are not robots and that all we need do in order to act rightly is to insert the appropriate data. Not only is man capable of deliberately acting against his judgment of conscience, it also appears that man, even if he has decided to act in accord with his conscientious judgment, may for some reason be unable to do so.

But if Paul's words are true, if they reflect genuine human experience, do they not seem to make a mockery of morality and call into absurdity all of our moral strivings? Can we really talk of morality at all if it is true that at times we find ourselves meaning to do one thing and then doing something else? Does acknowledgement of the experience to which Paul refers require us to accept Jean-Paul Sartre's view that all our moral strivings are ultimately "useless passions," doomed to frustration and failure?[27]

Something paradoxical, indeed something indicative of the depths of human existence, is at stake here—and something that is at the very heart of a Christian ethic. This paradox can make sense only if we admit that our moral lives are more complex and tension-filled than we frequently suppose. There seem to be operative in human existence factors that Macquarrie, in a magnificently perceptive passage, has called *disabling* or crippling as well as factors that are *enabling* or supportive. Our struggle to make our lives more human, to achieve the *bonum humanum,* is lived in a framework or context that contains both supportive and crippling elements.[28] We do not live as isolated entities, in a vacuum, but in a world wherein we find both support and non-support, indeed, a world wherein we find positive invitations to evil. We live, in other words, in a world of tension between sin (the disabling factors) and grace (the enabling factors), and because we live in this kind of world our meaning as moral beings, as responsible and free beings is profoundly affected. Our purpose now is not to grapple with the issues that this fact brings to the fore, for that will occupy us at length later on, but merely to indicate, in drawing this chapter on our conscientious growth into the human to a close, that dimensions of human existence perhaps unsuspected are disclosed when we reflect on our experiences as beings capable of violating our own deep-seated awareness of ourselves. Prior to investigating these dimensions, however, it will be useful to see how our deeds or acts are related to our moral being, to our being as persons who grow into the human, and to see more precisely what reality-making or truth-making factors are determinative of the humanness or inhumanness of our deeds.

Notes

1. Sigmund Freud, *An Outline of Psychoanalysis,* translated by James Strachey (London: Hogarth Press, 1949), pp. 3-4.

2. Robert White, *The Abnormal Personality* (New York: McGraw Hill, 1958), p. 38.

3. Lawrence Kohlberg, "Stages of Moral Development as a Basis for Moral Education," in *Moral Education: Interdisciplinary Approaches,* edited by C. M. Beck, B. S. Crittenden, and E. V. Sullivan (New York: Newman Press, 1971), p. 86.

4. *Ibid.,* p. 87.

5. See, for example, the illuminating article by Zilboorg, "Superego and Conscience," in *Conscience: Theological and Psychological Perspectives,* edited by C. Ellis Nelson (New York: Newman Press, 1973), pp. 210-223. Zilboorg's essay originally appeared in *Ministry and Medicine in Human Relations,* edited by Iago Galdstone, M.D. (New York: International Universities Press, Inc.; 1955), pp. 100-118. The anthology edited by Nelson is an excellent sourcebook on conscience.

6. John W. Glaser, "Conscience and Superego: A Key Distinction," in Nelson, *op. cit.*, pp. 175-176. Glaser's article originally appeared in *Theological Studies* 32 (1971) 30-47.

7. John Macquarrie, *Three Issues in Ethics* (New York: Harper & Row, 1970), p. 111. Macquarrie's chapter on conscience, entitled "Conscience, Sin and Grace" in his own book, is reprinted under the title "The Struggle of Conscience for Authentic Selfhood," in the Nelson anthology, pp. 155-166.

8. Macquarrie, *ibid.*, p. 111 (Nelson, p. 155).

9. Macquarrie, *ibid.* (Nelson, p. 155).

10. See above, p. 58.

11. On the notion of synderesis see the excellent study by Eric D'Arcy, *Conscience and Its Right to Freedom* (New York: Sheed and Ward, 1961), in particular, pp. 61-65.

12. Macquarrie, *ibid.*, p. 112 (Nelson, p. 156).

13. *Documents of Vatican II,* edited by Walter Abbott, S. J. (New York: Guild Press, 1965), "Pastoral Constitution on the Church in the Modern World," par. 16, p. 213.

14. Macquarrie, *ibid.*, p. 114 (Nelson, p. 158).

15. On the distinction between neurotic and authentic guilt see the essays by Paul Ricoeur ("Guilt, Ethics, and Religion," pp. 11-27), Zilboorg, and Martin Buber ("Guilt and Guilt Feelings," pp. 224-237) in the Nelson anthology.

16. See below, Chapter Five, pp. 113-138.

17. On the obligation to follow an erroneous conscience see St. Thomas Aquinas, *Summa Theologiae,* I-II, 6, 8; 19, 6. See also D'Arcy, *op. cit.*, pp. 110-111.

18. Albert Jonsen, *Christian Decision and Action* (New York: Bruce Publishing Company, 1970), pp. 141-142.

19. *Documents of Vatican II,* "Dogmatic Constitution on the Church;" par. 25, p. 18.

20. *Ibid.*, "Pastoral Constitution on the Church in the Modern World," par. 16, p. 213.

21. See note 17.

22. Richard A. McCormick, S. J., "Notes on Moral Theology," *Theological Studies* 29 (1958) 715-716.

23. Macquarrie, *op. cit.*, p. 117 (Nelson, p. 160).

24. Bernard Lonergan, *Method in Theology* (New York: Herder & Herder, 1972), p. 20 f.

25. On this see Albert Jonsen, *Responsibility in Modern Religious Ethics* (Washington: Corpus, 1968).

26. See Thomas Aquinas, *Summa Theologiae.*, 47, 8; see Josef Pieper, *The Four Cardinal Virtues* (Notre Dame, Ind.: University of Notre Dame Press, 1966), p. 8.

27. Jean-Paul Sartre, *Being and Nothingness,* translated by Hazel Barnes (New York: Philosophical Library, 1958), p. 608.

28. Macquarrie, *ibid.,* pp. 119-125 (Nelson, pp. 161-165).

Chapter Four:

BECOMING HUMAN IN AND
THROUGH OUR DEEDS

If ethics can properly be described as the endeavor to discover what it takes to make and keep human life human, and if we can meaningfully say that we "grow" into the human, that we can become "more" human than we actually are, then it is obvious that ethical inquiry must be deeply concerned with the meaning of human deeds, human acts. The reason why is simply that we make ourselves "more" or "less" human through those acts that we perform as intelligent and self-determinative beings, that is, through those acts that are called "human" or "moral" in order to distinguish them from those acts that we perform without thought or choice, such as breathing, blinking our eyelids, sneezing, or snoring.[1]

We are interested in human acts, human deeds, human behavior, not primarily in themselves—after all, they do not exist in themselves—but because they are clues to our identity; in other words, we are concerned with human deeds because it is in and through them that we both reveal who we are and become who we are to be.[2] At times we call these acts "good" or "bad," but we realize that it is actually the human person who is "good" or "bad," both disclosing himself as such and making himself to be such in and through his deeds.

Inquiry into human acts or thinking about them is what we mean by deliberation. This kind of inquiry is necessarily practical, that is, pointed to action, to what is-to-be done or is-not-to-be done. It is is-to-be thinking, of which "ought" thinking is a special mode,[3] as distinct from "is" thinking. It is a human activity carried out through what Aquinas and the Scholastics called "practical reason" or what we might today term human intelligence as order to action. It is, in short, a characteristic of men as intelligent beings capable of knowing what they are doing and why, capable of raising questions about the significance of their deeds, free to determine for themselves whether they shall act responsibly or not in accord with what they know to be the truth of the situation.[4]

To discover the meaning of our moral or human acts, we must be able to speak about them, to describe them, to question our lived experience as acting beings in order to objectify the intelligibility or meaning of this experience and to verify this meaning as reasonably warranted.[5] The task of describing properly our human acts is a central concern of ethics, and it is one common to the Christian and to anyone who is seriously seeking to understand the moral strivings of mankind. But to do this properly is not so easy as it might first appear, as Eric D'Arcy[6] and Paul Ramsey[7] have so clearly demonstrated in their critiques, respectively, of the "extreme" or "act" utilitarianism advocated by J. J. C. Smart and of the situationism or "new morality" that is so persuasively articulated by Joseph Fletcher.[8] D'Arcy and Ramsey, among others, note the very real danger to moral discourse that is rooted in our propensity to *redescribe* our acts in terms of their intended consequences—to justify, for instance, medical experiments involving risks concealed from subjects on the grounds that these experiments will advance medical technologies and eventually benefit great numbers of people. This propensity was strikingly revealed to the American people when persons responsible for burglarizing the private files of Daniel Ellsberg's psychiatrist and for other invasions of privacy defended their activities on the grounds that they were intended to defend the nation's security.

It might be suggested that the consequentialist type of ethics represented by Smart[9] and Fletcher and rejected by D'Arcy and Ramsey can be called an *ethics of intended good consequences* or an *ethics of intent* in order to distinguish it from what can be termed an *ethics of intent + content;* and our goal in this chapter will be to show that the second type of ethics is more open to reality, more responsive to the needs and claims of living persons, and more capable of helping us in our struggle to become human than the first.

For Smart, Fletcher, and others who incline, in various ways, to agree with them in their appraisal of the significance of human deeds, the overriding determinant of the rightness or wrongness of human acts is the good consequences that these acts will bring about, and these consequences are directly related to the agent's intent, for they tell us *why* he did what he did. Their attainment provides a sufficient or proportionate reason for doing deeds that one would not, as Fletcher is so fond of saying, "ordinarily and typically and usually" do,[10] for instance, rape, torture, kill, deceive. In other words the good consequences intended by the agent exercise the function, in this type of ethical analysis, of the *exception-making* criterion discussed by David Lyons in his study of utilitarianism[11] and so cogently analyzed by Ramsey in an important article called "The Case of the Curious Exception."[12] Ramsey puts the criterion negatively: Don't lie or cheat or steal or rape unless doing so is necessary in order to achieve the good articulated in the exception-making criterion. It is possible, I believe, to express this criterion affirmatively by saying: Do *anything* in order to achieve the good expressed in the criterion. And this is indeed precisely what Fletcher does, for he justifies any human activity, including genocide,[13] *if* the doing of this deed is judged necessary in order to do what he calls the human thing, the Christian thing, the loving thing, by which he means whatever will bring about the greatest good for the greatest number.

To put the matter somewhat differently, we can say that a consequentialist (or teleological, in the terminology of some writers) type of ethics describable as an ethics of intent is concerned with human acts to the extent that these acts *get something done*. It is interested in the *results* of our deeds and discovers their meaning or intelligibility in what they *do* to individuals and societies. An ethics of intent + content, on the other hand, although it is indeed interested in what our actions do, is also terribly concerned with our deeds to the extent that they *get something said,* to the degree that they play a role in human communication, in the life of dialogue to which we human beings are called. To see what I mean by this a passage from Herbert McCabe will prove helpful, for it is luminously clear. McCabe writes:

Ethics is just the study of human behaviour
insofar as it is a piece of communication, in-

sofar as it says something or fails to say something. This does not mean that ethics is uninterested in behaviour insofar as it gets something done, that ethics is not concerned with the consequences of my acts, but its precise concern is with my action as meaningful. The two, of course, are closely related. It is because of the effect on you of having a knife stuck into you that my act of knifing you has the *meaning* that it has. But the connection may be quite loose. A mother may smack her child very lightly and almost painlessly and the child will show that he recognizes the act as meaning some kind of rejection; on the other hand, in a game you may hit him much harder and he will be delighted by the sheer physical contact that means the opposite of rejection.[14]

An ethics of intent + content, consequently, is very much interested in factors *other than consequences* in properly describing or evaluating human acts. A workable model for describing human acts in an ethics of this kind is provided by a modified form of the approach, reaching back to Aristotle and formally developed by the Scholastics, that distinguishes between the object, the end, and the circumstances. This approach offers a workable model because it raises the questions that must be raised in any attempt to describe properly the meaning of our human deeds, in any effort to reflect critically on the true meaning of our moral experience. The approach cannot be mechanistically or wooden-headedly adopted (for this engenders the externalistic, legalistic approach so roundly and rightly criticized by Fletcher); it must be imaginatively and creatively adapted for the simple reason that our experiences open new horizons to us and raise new kinds of questions so that we must constantly search for the *true meaning* behind old questions and answers in our struggle to understand our existence as moral beings. Yet this approach does give us a framework for truthfully and properly describing our human deeds. Perhaps the basic flaw in the *use* of this approach in the traditional natural-law position of Roman Catholic moralists was a tendency to look at the act and reach a moral judgment too quickly on the basis of its *physical* description and by a failure on the part of some to recognize that "circumstances" could inwardly modify or change the very meaning of the act itself as a human deed.

At any rate, we can say that this approach consists basically in asking questions about our acts as realities that consist *in* the relationships that they establish between a human being as a moral agent and the human world in which he lives and acts. The relevant questions for an ethics of intent + content seem to be the following: (1) *What* is the act or behavior doing? Here we quickly realize that a purely physical description of a piece of behavior is not the "what" we are seeking, for its moral or human significance is not discoverable simply from an analysis of its physical structure, although this structure does provide us with indispensable clues. For instance, what is the moral significance of inserting a hypodermic needle into the flesh of a living human being? We cannot tell unless we know more about the act. In order to know more we have to know who is doing the inserting, into whom the needle is being inserted, why it is being inserted, etc. Thus we need to ask (2) *Who* is acting? (3) *To whom* or *in whom* is the act being done? (4) *How* is it being done? (5) *When* is it being done? (6) *Where* is it being done? and (7) *Why* is it being done? In addition, we can ask whether any alternatives to the act in question exist or whether this particular act is the only conceivable means currently possible for securing a given end, and we can also inquire into the foreseeable consequences of the act, both short-range and long-run. All these factors enter into the total moral situation. Because the line between act and consequences is fluid, it is possible sometimes to describe the act itself in terms of its consequences; but this is not, as D'Arcy has argued so cogently,[15] possible at all times if one is going to be truthful in his description of a given act. Since this is so, it seems better to limit the expression *human act* or *moral act* in its more precise and restricted sense to the total ensemble minus consequences and alternatives. Still, in evaluating the moral situation as a whole and in reaching a conscientious judgment about the humanness or inhumanness of the act itself, these consequences and alternatives must be taken into account.

In addition, it is imperative to ask ourselves, in properly describing our human deeds, whether any right will be violated by the act or, conversely, whether any wrong will be done either to ourselves or to other human beings. The fact that a wrong will be done and a right violated—that is, the fact that some human being or human beings will be wronged because of the act—does not necessarily mean that the act ought not be done, yet this does make us realize that certain conditions or truth-making factors must be present in order to justify or warrant the doing of a wronging but not wrongful deed.

It is not difficult to see the pertinence of these questions. Long ago Thomas Aquinas noted the difference between the natural species or classification of an act (a description of it in terms of its physical structure and results) and the moral species of an act. Obviously an act having the same physical description or natural species can belong to several moral species, depending on the answers that have to be given to the questions that must be raised. The physical act of spanking a child, for instance, may be morally an act of vintage rage, child abuse, or loving correction. Sexual intercourse may be an act expressing marital love, incest, bestiality, egoistic self-gratification.[16] The who, where, when, how, why, and so forth afford us the clues that we must follow if we are to be responsive to what Lonergan terms the "transcendental precepts" of being attentive to experience, intelligent in seeking its meaning, reasonable in testing the truth of this meaning, and responsible in acting.[17] They put us in lived contact with the relational and real factors that go to make up our deeds as expressions of our moral being, of our humanity.

In raising these questions and attempting to answer them, men seek to discover the meaning of their moral experience and to articulate in an objective way (so that human discourse is possible) their spontaneous effort to understand this experience, and to verify their understanding of it. There is no basic argument over the first normative or regulative principle of our moral life, namely that good is to be done and evil is to be avoided. This is one of the truths of understanding that we discussed in the second chapter in our consideration of knowing the human. Although controversies rage over the meaning of the good in any concrete or specific sense, I believe that the position outlined in the first chapter, where I expressed my agreement with many moralists that the human good is pluriform—that is, that it refers to a set of goods or values that actually do correspond to genuine human needs and that define in meaningful ways basic dimensions of the human person—is not only true but eminently reasonable and, as indicated in the first chapter, in harmony with a biblical perspective.[18] These real goods function, as we have seen, as principles of intelligent activity—of practical reason, as the Scholastics put it,[19] or as guides to choice in the terminology of the developmental psychologist Lawrence Kohlberg,[20] or as *directions of action* (as opposed to *directives of action*) in the language of Paul Ramsey.[21] Each real human good (e.g., life itself, health, friendship, justice, etc.) is a good to be prized, not priced; is a good that opens up authentic possibilities of human existence.[22] And man's *moral* good, that is, his worth as a man and not as a cook or athlete or theologian or politician, is fundamentally related to his attitude toward the entire complexus of the *bonum humanum* and struggle to pursue it.[23]

If we now look at the various moral rules that have been developed by human beings in their attempt to express in more specific and defined ways the meaning of their moral existence (e.g., don't kill, don't steal, don't commit adultery, don't lie), we will realize that these rules are intended to specify more precisely the attitude that must be expressed in actions if human beings are going to respond truthfully and rightfully to the appeals made to them by the real human and personal goods that together constitute the *bonum humanum* and that function in our consciousness, as we have seen already, as the general guides to our choices. These rules are not, as Fletcher would have them, purely prudential maxims summarizing a "wisdom" generated by a consequentialist calculus of the consequences that men have previously experienced as a result of human deeds.[24] Rather they are the fruit of a responsible reflection on the meaning of man's moral experience and attempt to state in specifiable ways the types of activities that do in fact enhance or destroy basic human goods. These rules, which ultimately are rooted in a human love for the human good in its totality, were worked out by raising the kinds of questions that we have said must be raised if we are to make sense of our moral experience.

Since these questions are given shape by the existential situations in which they are raised, it is necessary to keep raising them and in this way to see more clearly what goods and human meanings are and how they can best be brought into existence and protected. The search for the human is an on-going quest, for the "human," like "love," is a "growing" word,[25] but the quest is not absurd, for it has direction and continuity.

Because the quest is on-going, however, it is reasonable to expect that most moral rules (with the exception of those that identify modes of human behavior that one can rightly write off as atrocious) are open to revision. The manner of their revision has, I believe, been quite well described by Paul Ramsey in his discussion of the function of exempting conditions and qualifying conditions,[26] and there is no need to retrace the thinking so well set forth in the writings of Ramsey, Joseph Fuchs,[27] Bernard Häring,[28] and others with regard to this question.

Yet it is important, primarily because of a direction discernible in recent writings by moralists, principally Catholic theologians working out of a natural-law tradition, to look carefully at the question of intent, or *why,* and its role in evaluating the human meaning of our acts. In reflecting on the issues brought to light by raising this question, we come to grips with the meaning of man's human acts as these are related to his moral being; that is, we see in a fresh and more perceptive manner the way in which our personal identity is both disclosed in and through our deeds and shaped in and through them.

When we ask why an action is done, we are led to

the important consideration of the role played by intention as a determinant of the rightness or wrongness of our deeds. Clearly the agent's intent plays a major role here, and a few brief comments will illustrate why. To aid someone in distress is usually regarded, for instance, as a kind or friendly act, the "human" thing to do. But if the person coming to the help of another has in mind or intends some ulterior motive (the *finis operantis* of the Scholastics), perhaps winning the other's confidence so that he can be duped into something or betrayed in some way, the entire act is put into a new perspective. Likewise, to sever a person's arm is an act that can have many meanings, largely dependent on the agent's intention. It would be mayhem or mutilation or torture if the person doing it were doing so out of spite or hatred or in an attempt to gain information, but it would be an element or partial aspect of an act of saving life if the arm were severed so that the person, trapped under a burning car, could be removed to safety. Similarly, for a physician to examine a female patient for breast lumps is morally right, even if the physician knows beforehand that in examining this particular patient he is going to experience erotic sensations. But if the physician examined a female patient for breast lumps *in order to* have erotic sensations his action would have an entirely different meaning and would be properly describable not as an act of examining a patient but as an act of sexual exploitation.

The key role played by intent in evaluating the moral worth of a human act and in governing the proper way to describe morally a given deed is widely recognized and has been reflected in several recent attempts, among them those of Peter Knauer[29] and Germain Grisez,[30] to rethink the meaning of direct and indirect intention, particularly as this is spelled out in the principle of double effect. The problem can be formulated by saying that there are many times in our lives when our actions will inevitably cause evil, that is, the loss of physical health, pain, injustice, even death. To put it another way, we are sometimes so situated that no matter what we do we are going to "wrong" others. The more traditional and commonly accepted view was that we could rightly do something that inescapably causes evil (wrongs some human beings) only if we directly intended the good that also issued from the act, merely permitting or indirectly intending the evil consequence or consequences of the act, and only if the good achieved by the action was not attained by means of the evil.[31] There is, however, a growing tendency among several important contemporary writers to reject the principle of double effect and—in my judgment this is something far more significant—the distinction between the directly intended and the indirectly intended that makes the principle intelligible, and to contend that this distinction is basically a matter of moral quibbling and, as one writer puts it,[32] simply a casuistic desire to "save" consciences. For these writers a more honest, that is, truthful way of understanding the dilemmas experienced when we were in situations of the nature previously described, is to say that we *directly* intend the evil we bring about, but that there is a proportionate reason, discernible in the good also intended and effected, for undertaking the action in question and that this reason (i.e., the intended good consequence) is the factor that morally legitimates the act. Among those who endorse this tendency can be included William Van der Marck,[33] Cornelius Van der Poel,[34] and Bruno Schüller.[35] Van der Poel, for example, writes as follows: "in the killing of a human being, the issue is not whether the person who is going to be killed is guilty or innocent,

90

nor whether the killing is direct or indirect; the question, rather, is what kind of human self-realization is taking place and what is the interpersonal impact of this action."[36]

The line of thought common to these writers has been clearly set forth—and to a very large measure endorsed and accepted—by Richard McCormick, a Jesuit, who is surely one of the leading moralists within the Catholic community in the United States and whose superlative summaries and commentaries on moral literature are a regular feature of *Theological Studies* and place everyone interested in understanding man's struggle to become human in his debt. Perhaps the clearest presentation of the position is provided in his discussion of two articles by Schüller[37] and a major article by Fuchs[38] (whom McCormick believes to be basically in agreement with the position developed but who is not necessarily, as I will indicate later, rightly to be numbered among those who accept the position McCormick describes). This exposition is found in one of McCormick's "Notes on Moral Theology"[39] and is later expanded by him in his 1973 Pere Marquette Lecture in Theology.[40] In his earlier presentation, McCormick first notes that both Schüller and Fuchs sharply distinguish *nonmoral* (Schüller's term) or *premoral* (Fuchs' term) evil from *moral* evil, or between *evil* and *wickedness* (and this is a distinction that is, I believe, justified and acknowledged either explicitly or implicitly by a great many writers). For instance, to use examples advanced by Fuchs,[41] killing, wounding, deceiving, and sterilizing are evil insofar as they destroy a good that is one of the real components of the *bonum humanum*. Yet we can still ask whether killing, wounding, deceiving, and sterilizing are morally evil or wicked. The use of the gerund here may be unfortunate, for it implies that

91

what is being discussed is the human act in question, namely, an act of killing or wounding or deceiving or sterilizing. It would probably be more accurate if the instances offered by Fuchs of premoral evil would be expressed in terms of the injurious, wronging, or evil results of the acts, in these cases death, injury, deception, and sterilization, and later on I will try to make my reasons clear for preferring this way of speaking. For the present, however, I think that the major point stressed by Schüller and Fuchs and endorsed by McCormick is correct, namely that there is a difference between premoral or nonmoral evil and moral evil. What these writers mean (and this is also an element common to the analyses of Van der Marck and Van der Poel) is that moral evil arises *only* when the evil involved in an act is endorsed, ratified, and accepted by the agent.

Yet, as noted previously, in some situations it is inevitable that we cause evil, and the evil caused is related to our intentions and, through our intentions, to our moral being. McCormick, summarizing the direction he discovers in the thought of Schüller and Fuchs (and his summary applies equally to the work of Van der Marck and Van der Poel, as his later Pere Marquette Lecture makes clear), believes that it can be expressed most clearly as follows:

Would it not be clearer and more precise to say that it is legitimate to intend premoral evil *in ordine ad finem proportionatum*? I may choose and intend the pain of a child or a patient if it is the only way or the most reasonable way to secure his greater good. The "greater good" does not mean that the premoral disvalue is not intended; it means that it is not intended *propter se*. Therefore, would it not be better to say that it is legitimate to intend a disvalue *in se sed non propter se?* When there is no proportionate reason, the disvalue caused is chosen and intended *in se et propter se,* and it is this *propter se* which makes the act immoral. I believe that this is what Fuchs means by "intending evil *as such*," but his occasional use of the simple and unqualified word "intend" leaves the matter a bit murky.[42]

It is fair to say, in short, that Schüller, Van der Marck, Van der Poel and McCormick agree that it is morally right to intend and effect a nonmoral or premoral evil if there is a sufficient or proportionate reason for intending and effecting such evil. For them the proportionate reason (=the greater good intended) is a reality- or truth-making factor whose presence in a moral situation *alone* justifies a deed that "wrongs" others by effecting an evil that is properly intended by the doer. Although McCormick does not, as do Van der Poel and Van der Marck, reject the distinction between the directly intended and the indirectly intended,[43] nor limit it, as does Schüller, to situations in which scandal is concerned,[44] he correctly identifies the major thrust of their writings and accepts this thrust, for he writes:

where a higher good is at stake and the only *means* to protect it is to choose to do a nonmoral evil, then the will remains properly disposed to the values constitutive of human good. . . This is to say that the intentionality is good even when the person, reluctantly and regretfully to be sure, intends the non-moral evil if a truly proportionate reason for such a choice is present.[45]

Fuchs' position, as McCormick indicates, is somewhat ambiguous. It may be that he would agree with McCormick's way of interpreting his position, but there are aspects of his thought that point in a different direction. By looking at these elements of Fuchs' thought we can, I believe, get to the heart of the issue in this entire subject of intention and its relationship to the moral value of our deeds. It will help first to look at the way Fuchs describes the situation and McCormick's comments on Fuchs' position; next we can profitably review briefly some ideas developed by Germain Grisez and Paul Ramsey that bear on the question; and finally we can conclude with some personal observations in the hope that the analysis provided will enable readers to understand why this is an exceptionally critical subject for human beings.

Fuchs, after distinguishing between premoral and moral evil, asks when a man in his human action is morally good. His reply is that a man is morally good

when he *intends and effects* a human good (value)—in the premoral sense, for example, life, health, joy, culture, etc. . . . but not when he *has in view and effects* a human non-good, an evil (nonvalue)—in the premoral sense, for example, death, wounding, wrong, etc. What if he intends and effects good, but this necessarily involves effecting evil also? We answer, if the realization of the evil through the intended realization of good is justified as a proportionally related cause, then in this case only good was intended. Man has almost always judged in this manner.[46]

At first glance this statement seems to be quite conformable to the position so clearly presented by McCormick. Yet we should note that Fuchs insists that *only* the good was intended in an action having evil consequences as well as good consequences that function as a "proportionally related cause." He refuses to say, as McCormick says, that the evil effected was intended in any moral sense or that "what was and is decisive [in actions effecting evil] is the proportionate reason for acting."[47] In addition, Fuchs insists that the evil consequences inevitably issuing from the act must be a part or element of *one* human act.[48] He is saying, in effect, that the act must be describable as one ordered of itself (that has as its *finis operis*, to adopt the terminology of the Scholastics) to the good, e.g., a surgical operation, a physical examination, legitimate defense, and that the act is itself the *means* to the end. In other words, he is implying that the evil associated with the act is not to be regarded as a means but as a partial aspect of one entire act, and that this act is itself the means.

It is instructive to note that McCormick, in commenting on Fuchs' views, is worried by his requirement that the act be describable as *one* act. He rightly observes that "there are two elements Fuchs appeals to in justifying the doing of premoral evil: proportionate reason and the fact that the evil is simply an element of one human action."[49] He then continues: "Perhaps Fuchs' insistence that the premoral evil be incorporated into the one act overstates the requirements a bit. However this may be, such insistence either (1) very sharply limits the premoral evils one may cause in the pursuit of good or (2) expands the notion of 'one human action' to the point where human language will no longer sustain the unity."[50]

I believe that McCormick, with the perception that one has come to expect of him, has touched on the crucial point in this comment. Whereas McCormick voices dissatisfaction with Fuchs' demand for the unity of the act,[51] I believe that he is contributing an exceptionally important insight in making this demand. Of the two alternatives McCormick poses if we do insist on the unity of the act, the first is surely the one that should be adopted. The claim that an act causing evil as well as good must be describable as one human act certainly does limit severely the "premoral evils one may cause in the pursuit of good," and it has great significance for the validity of the distinction between the directly intended and the indirectly intended. I suggest that this condition rescues any position justifying the doing of evil for a proportionate good from becoming a position willing to make the good sought an exception-making criterion. It saves one's ethical position from slipping into a consequentialist ethic of intent. In other words, I believe that the tendency to justify the effecting of evil *solely* in terms of a proportionate reason (the *finis proportionatus* stipulated by McCormick) *can be* a tendency to build into one's methodology the exception-making criterion that eviscerates all the human experience and inquiry that has gone on in man's search to understand the meaning of his moral experience and to objectify this understanding in defined-action rules. This criterion is precisely the good chosen as the proportionate reason for performing the act; it is the good that now serves as the sole principle of intelligent activity, before which other human goods must bow. If a particular human good actually does perform this function in one's approach to judging moral situations, it means that one has opted for an ethics of intent only, for the good chosen as the proportionate reason is exactly what the agent intends to bring into being through his act. In other words, in justifying the doing of evil in an ethics that pays heed to content as well as to intent, *more than* a proportionate reason (i.e., a good achieved as a consequence of the act) is needed. This "more than," in addition, is what is at stake in the debate over the directly and the indirectly intended, that is, over the way the evil caused by the agent is brought within the scope of his intent, and this "more than" is brought sharply into focus in our endeavor to discover the unity of the act.

The point I am trying to make can be clarified if we look at the way in which the consequences of our actions are related to our moral being, to our intentions, to what we "have in view" in acting. Here it is instructive to cite McCormick once more, for I believe that he prejudices the issue in his description of the way acts are related to the agent's intentions. His analysis of the origin of the direct-indirect terminology is quite revealing in this regard. He writes:

Whenever one chooses to do a good, he leaves another undone. Right reason tells us that we may choose to pursue this good of our neighbor [why not of ourselves too, or is it wrong to pursue a good for ourselves?] only if it is at least as beneficial to him as the value we leave undone. This same analysis began to be applied also to the instance where human action caused a disvalue in a positive way, not simply by omission. Concretely, if some important value or good could be effected only by causing simultaneously some measure of harm, then that was judged morally proper if the good chosen was at least as important as the harm unavoidably caused. In other words there was a proportionate reason for *choosing the disvalue* (emphasis added). The disvalue was not to be imputed to me precisely because it was unavoidable.[52]

Note that McCormick says that we choose the dis-value. This statement can be challenged, and ought to be, for to accept this way of putting the matter is to prejudge the issue of direct vs. indirect intent. For instance, when he provides some specific examples McCormick says that "when one administers physical punishment to a refractory child from purely pedagogical motives, should we call the punishment and pain 'indirect'? Hardly. Rather it has the character of means and we speak of an intending will, a direct choice where means are concerned."[53] It is quite true that in the example cited by McCormick there is an intending will and direct choice of means. The *means* chosen, however, is *not* the pain and punishment suffered by the child, but is rather the *act* of administering physical punishment. We do not, I believe, properly *intend* the punishing pain in an instance of this kind but rather *foresee* that our act of correction will inevitably bring about pain, and to foresee is not necessarily to intend. Here some comments of Germain Grisez are pertinent:

Some authors seem to suppose that all foreseen effects of one's behavior are intended so long as they are accepted, however reluc-tantly, as the concomitants of the execution of one's objective. But this position conflicts with our ordinary-language use of the word 'intentional.' . . . When I go to the dentist, I foresee that I shall suffer pain, but I do not intend the pain . . .[54]

To return to McCormick's example. If I spank a child (and as a father I have had occasion to do this) my act is an act of spite or vindictiveness if my proper intent (what I "have in view," to use Fuchs' language) is to cause pain—and, unfortunately, this has been the case at times. But if my intent is to correct, if I am motivated by pedagogical purposes, my act, morally speaking, is an act of correction. Similarly, as Grisez—and Aquinas for that matter—shows quite clearly, an act of self-defense may bring death to an assailant, and may be infallibly foreseen by the agent to result in death, yet the act is not an act properly describable as one of killing but is accurately and truthfully describable as an act of self-defense, although it may become an act of killing if the death of the assailant itself enters into the scope of the agent's intent.[55] Because Grisez has so well developed the difference between foreseeing and intending, there is no need to dwell on it here. Neither do I want to over-simplify matters nor to suggest that one go through a tortuous process of psychological analysis, for I realize that quite frequently it is very difficult, if not impossible, for a person to know just what his intentions are—and Paul's words in Romans 7:15 ff are pertinent here. Still it does make a real difference to one's moral being whether he actually does intend the evil as such (*in se*, as McCormick puts it[56]), that is, directly, or not, for it indicates the extent to which a person ratifies and says yes to the evil that he effects.

Grisez, in his rethinking of the question of the directly and the indirectly intended, stresses that one may do a deed that inevitably results in evil consequences *only* if the act can properly be described as *one* human act that is in itself ordered to the good. Here he is in agreement with Fuchs, but in addition he offers suggestions concerning the unity of the act that merit reflection—indeed, McCormick accepts in a tentative way the conditions that Grisez lays down for determining the unity of a moral act, although he then goes on to argue that even if the act is unified in this way it can be directly ordered to effecting evil if a proportionate reason is present.[57] Grisez argues that a human act is unified or *one* by reason of two factors. The first is the unity of the agent's intention, and by this he means not only the end willed by the agent but also the meaning that the agent understands his act to have when he chooses it as a means to his intended end. The other is the indivisibility of the performance *as this performance is related to the capacity of the agent.* His understanding of this second source of an act's unity is set forth as follows:

A performance may be divisible by thought or divisible in the sense that under some other conditions it could be divided, yet remain practically indivisible for a given agent here and now. Obviously, so far as the performance affects the unity of a human act, the indivisibility that is relevant is that which is defined in terms of the actual power of the agent. If I cannot here and now divide my performance, then no sort of complexity within it can in and of itself determine my action to a multiplicity corresponding to that complexity.[58]

He then concludes that an act that is one both by reason of intention and by reason of the indivisibility of the performance is one in the strict sense and is to be described by the scope of the agent's intention and not by parts of the action that is as such and as a whole indivisible by the agent. Thus an act of self-defense is not describable as an act of killing if it is in fact intended to be an act of self-defense and if the actual performance or use of counterforce by the agent is an indivisible act on his part. In such an act, the death of an assailant (if this actually does occur, and even if it is foreseen to occur) is not the *means* to the end of self-defense, but is a partial aspect or element of the counterforce employed.[59]

100

It is here that some observations of Ramsey are pertinent. Although Ramsey differs in some significant ways from Grisez in his analysis of the meaning of our human acts,[60] there are important similarities between the two;[61] furthermore, Ramsey calls to attention something that is of the utmost significance, I believe, in our consideration of the validity of the distinction between the directly intended and the indirectly intended. Ramsey sharply distinguishes between the *motives* of the agent and the *intention* of the action, or what he also calls its "thrust" or "direction," a distinction that echoes, as Ramsey himself observes, the old Scholastic distinction between the *finis operantis* and the *finis operis*. His point is that we may rightly do something that does in fact bring about evil if our motives are upright, if there is a proportionate reason, *and* if the thrust or intention or direction of the action itself is primarily targeted upon the good that is achievable through the action and not upon the evil that inevitably and inescapably comes about through the action. As an example he cites instances when an abortion is required in order to save the mother's life. In these instances, he writes,

The intention of the action, and in this sense its direction, is not upon the *death* of the fetus, any more than are the motives of the agent. The intention of the action is directed upon the *incapacitation* of the fetus from doing what it is doing to the life of the mother, and is not directed toward the death of the fetus, as such, even in the killing of it . . . in this situation, it is correct to say that the intention of the action is not the killing, not the death of the fetus, but the incapacitation of it . . .[62]

How does this distinction between the intention or thrust of the action and the motives of the agent relate to the distinction between the directly intended and the indirectly intended? I believe that it relates in the following way. The thrust or intention of or direction of our deeds is one of the truth-making or reality-making factors that enter into the total moral situation. It is an intelligibly discernible feature of our acts. If the thrust or intention of a deed that we do is directly and primarily ordered to effecting evil, the doer of the deed cannot *not* intend the evil that it achieves. This evil is inescapably within the scope of his intention; it is not merely foreseen but is morally intended. The evil may be *unwanted*; and obviously it *ought to* be unwanted; it may be accepted only reluctantly and only for the sake of a good that will result as a consequence of the deed (McCormick's intending it *in se sed non propter se*), but it is accepted *and endorsed* by the agent, ratified by him, willingly though reluctantly incorporated by him into his moral being. In accepting it and in ratifying it the doer shows his willingness to take on, as part of his moral identity, the doer of evil. On the other hand, if the primary thrust or direction of the action itself is toward the good that is achievable in and through the deed and only indirectly toward the evil inescapably associated with the good that is accomplished, then the evil need not be the object of the agent's intention. It does not enter properly into the scope of his intention. In both instances we are speaking of *one* human act, and it is this act that is the means we choose in order to achieve the ends that serve as our motives in acting. But in the former instance the means or act we chose is evil because it directly bears on a destruction of a real human good that we cannot not intend to destroy, whereas in the second instance the means or act we choose is good because it directly bears on the good that the action is capable of achieving and only indirectly on the evil that likewise ensues and this evil, although foreseen, is not properly intended.

In developing his position Grisez reminds us of an analysis of human acts given by Thomas Aquinas. Since this Thomistic analysis is highly significant for understanding the difference between what I have termed an ethics of intent only as opposed to an ethics of intent + content, it will be appropriate to cite it here and to offer some comments concerning it. Aquinas wrote:

A twofold goodness or malice can be noted in the external act: one is derived from its fitting matter and circumstances; the other is derived from its order to an end. Now certainly the goodness derived from its order to an end depends totally on the will. But the goodness deriving from fitting matter and circumstances depends on reason: and the goodness of the will itself depends on this, to the extent that the will bears on it. But in order for anything to be evil it suffices that there is only one defect; in order for anything to be completely good one individual aspect of good is not enough but an integrity of goodness is required. Therefore if the will is good both from its proper object and from the end it follows that the external act is good. But it is not enough, in order that the external act be good, that there be the goodness of the will which is free from the intention of the end; but if the will is evil either from the end intended or from the act willed, it follows that the external act is evil.[63]

I believe that what Aquinas calls the "fitting matter and circumstances" can be called the *content* of
an act, whereas what he calls the order of the act to
its end can be called its *intent,* and that this intent is
obviously related to the consequences of the act. But
Thomas insists that the goodness of the will itself
(and it is the will that is involved in "intentions") is
dependent on the goodness of the "fitting matter and
circumstances" (what I call "content"), and that this
goodness is discoverable by intelligent inquiry. This
goodness, in other words, is dependent on the *real
relations* that link the act to the human world, that
actually *constitute* the act as a humanly significant
piece of behavior, as something that gets something
said in addition to getting something *done.* And among
these real relations is the intention or thrust of the
activity itself.

This goodness stemming from the content of the
act is likewise part of what we mean by the unity of
the act as a performance indivisible by the agent
himself. By this I mean that this source of the goodness of the act (its *content*) specifies the performance
in such a way that the agent cannot not intend the act
to have the meaning that it has. Here some examples
will be helpful. We may intend (in the sense of having
as our motive) our act to have one meaning that it
simply cannot have if we are truthful to the realities
that are involved. For instance, we may wish to make
the world a better place by ridding it of a dictator or
power-mad figure, such as Hitler or a dope
peddler; and we may wish to describe an act of assas-
sinating a person of this kind as an act of saving the
world or eliminating some evil force from our community. We may, to use an example of Van der Poel,
want to prevent a great deal of human suffering and
to enable individuals and society to develop by abort-
ing a defective fetus. Yet the acts in question in both

instances can truthfully be described as acts of assassination and of killing or feticide, and as such they are directly ordered against the good of life itself. The acts themselves are the means to intended ends, and the deaths of a power- or money-hungry figure and of a human fetus are directly the means to the end; they are not parts or elements of one total act of saving humanity or of preventing human suffering. Their deaths cannot be nonintended, and they cannot be nonintended precisely because their deaths are the "target" toward which the actions themselves are primarily directed.

A question of crucial moral significance is at stake in the way we describe our human acts and relate them to our personal identity through our intentions. There is, I am convinced, a terrible danger in the tendency among many contemporary moralists, in particular Catholic theologians, to claim that we can rightfully intend or will evil *in se in ordine ad finem proportionatum,* a danger of incorporating into their ethical methodology an exception-making criterion and, by so doing, of turning their ethics into an ethics of intent only, an ethics ultimately justifiable in terms of some overridingly important human good that can be achieved as a consequence of the deed.

Neither Van der Marck, Van der Poel, Schüller, nor McCormick really wants to build an exception-making criterion into his methodology.[64] Yet all of their analyses of human acts are logically open to such a criterion. The "building up of community" that Van der Marck erects into the ultimate norm of distinguishing right from wrong and "the impact on the individual and society" that Van der Poel characterizes as the ultimate criterion can certainly justify directly doing acts that, properly described, are not acts with both good and evil consequences but acts whose ultimate effect is good, although their immediate and direct aim is the willed destruction of some real human good in a real human being. Likewise McCormick insists that the evil we do is ultimately justifiable "if a genuinely proportionate reason . . . is present," and this proportionate reason is some specific human good that is of a "higher" order or value than the good destroyed.[65] But the basic human goods, such as life, health, justice, friendship, peace, simply cannot be measured off one against another. None is an absolute—and this is what the "higher" good becomes in McCormick's position—in the sense that it is of such overriding importance that other basic human goods can be directly judged evil here and now and not worth protection.

In summary, the consequentialist type of ethics that is willing to justify the doing of evil for the sake of a higher good ignores the content of the act as a human deed that has a human significance and meaning independent of its consequences and the motives of the agent. It is an ethics that, when the chips are down, sees human acts simply as ways of getting things done, of achieving results, and fails to see their reality as communicative and intelligible units of human "language," as expressive or manifestive of what it means to be human.

The reflections offered here in describing human deeds do not, of course, do justice to the immense complexity of man's moral life and the significance of his acts. Human beings are not pure intelligences, nor is human behavior capable of being completely grasped by reason. There are non-cognitive, infra- and supra-rational elements that enter into human action, and the moralist, in particular the Christian moralist, must ponder seriously the meaning of Paul's words in Romans 7:15-19: "I do not understand my own actions. The good that I will I do not, whereas the evil that I hate, that I do." Still an intelligent analysis of human acts forces us to admit that we cannot properly evaluate moral situations unless we open our minds to the content (fitting matter and circumstances) as well as to the intent. To put it somewhat differently, an intelligent analysis leads us to agree with Ramsey that agapeic love (or humanitarian justice) is not only a motivation or objective for actions but is also structured, that is, built into the acts that persons do, so that it is quite possible—indeed certain—that some kinds of deeds simply cannot count as expressions of agape, as expressions of the human.[66]

Notes

1. The distinction between *human acts,* which alone are the subject of moral evaluation, and what older writers called "acts of man" is classical. A basic statement on this distinction is found in Thomas Aquinas, *Summa theologiae,* 1-2, 1, 1.

2. On this see Herbert McCabe, *What Is Ethics All About?* (Washington: Corpus, 1969), pp. 90-94.

3. On the distinction between "is-to-be" thinking and "ought" thinking see the discussion in Chapter 2, above, pp. 25-49.

4. On this see Thomas Aquinas, *Summa theologiae,* 1, q. 79, a. 12; 1-2, q. 94, a. 2. See also Germain Grisez, *Contraception and the Natural Law* (Milwaukee: Bruce Publishing Company, 1964), pp. 60-66; idem, *Abortion: The Myths, the Realities, and the Arguments* (New York: Corpus, 1970), pp. 310-325.

5. On this see Bernard J. F. Lonergan, *Method in Theology* (New York: Herder and Herder, 1972), pp. 11-12.

6. Eric D'Arcy, *Human Acts: An Essay in Their Moral Evaluation* (Oxford: Oxford University Press, 1963), pp. 1-40. Note in particular the third thesis defended by D'Arcy on p. 18 ff: "Certain kinds of acts are of such significance that the terms which denote them may not, special contexts apart, be elided into terms which (a) denote their consequences and (b) conceal, or even fail to reveal, the nature of the act itself." D'Arcy discusses Smart's views on pp. 2-3.

7. Paul Ramsey, *Deeds and Rules in Christian Ethics* (New York: Scribner's, 1967), pp. 192-225.

8. The situationism of Fletcher and its affinities to utilitarianism are discussed perceptively by Grisez, *Abortion* . . ., pp. 287-296.

9. Smart represents what has been called "extreme" or "act" utilitarianism, as distinguished from "rule utilitarianism." A good collection of essays representing both types in their varied and "mixed" forms is provided by Michael D. Bayles, *Contemporary Utilitarianism* (New York: Doubleday Anchor Books, 1968).

10. See, for example, Joseph Fletcher and Thomas Wassmer, *Hello, Lovers: An Invitation to Situation Ethics* (New York: Corpus, 1970), p. 8.

11. David Lyons, *The Forms and Limits of Utilitarianism* (Oxford: Oxford University Press, 1965), p. 125.

12. Paul Ramsey, "The Case of the Curious Exception," in Gene Outka and Paul Ramsey, editors, *Norm and Context in Christian Ethics* (New York: Scribner's, 1968), pp. 82-93. On p. 86 Ramsey states: "The fact is that if one attaches an exception-making criterion at any point along a line of reasoning from the more general to the more specific principles, all the moral insight that went before the scale is immediately suspended."

13. For Fletcher's justification of genocide see *Hello, Lovers*, pp. 76-77.

14. McCabe, *op. cit.*, p. 92.

15. D'Arcy, *op. cit.*, pp. 18-25.

16. On this, see Thomas Aquinas, *Summa theologiae*, 1-2, 1, 3, ad 3: "It is possible for an act of one physical kind (*unus actus secundum speciem naturae*) to be willed for diverse ends: for instance the taking of human life considered as a physical event is generically always the same (*idem secundum speciem naturae*), yet considered as a moral act it can be of specifically different kinds when the purpose is upholding justice or when satisfying anger: one is an act of virtue, the other an act of vice. Now an action receives its specific character (*speciem*) from a term that is essential to it (*per se*), not incidental (*per accidens*). Moral purposes lie outside merely natural processes, and conversely the purpose there does not constitute moral situations. And so there is nothing to stop acts of the same physical category from belonging to diverse moral categories, and vice versa."

17. Lonergan, *op. cit.*, p. 20.

18. See Chapter One, above, pp. 1-22.

19. See, for instance, *Summa theologiae*, 1-2, 79, 12.

20. Lawrence Kohlberg, "Stages of Moral Development as a Basis for Moral Education," in C. M. Beck. B. S. Crittenden, and E. V. Sullivan, editors, *Moral Education: Interdisciplinary Approaches* (New York: Newman, 1971), p. 58 f. See above, Chapter Two, pp. 25-49.

21. Ramsey, "The Case of the Curious Exception," *loc. cit.*, p. 75.

22. For a very illuminating account of this aspect of real goods see Grisez, "Toward a Consistent Natural-Law Ethics of Killing," *The American Journal of Jurisprudence* 15 (1970) 69-70.

23. The emphasis by moral philosophers like Grisez and by moral theologians like Fuchs on the need for a basically moral *attitude* toward real human goods is one way of saying what the prophets of Israel and Jesus said about the need in man for a clean heart, a heart open to the full richness of human existence.

24. Fletcher, *Situation Ethics* (Philadelphia: Westminster, 1965), pp. 31-37, and "What's in a Rule? A Situationist's View," in Outka and Ramsey, editors, *Norm and Context in Christian Ethics*, pp. 325-349.

25. On this see the masterful discussion of love as a growing word in McCabe, *op. cit.*, pp. 18-30.

26. Ramsey, "The Case of the Curious Exception," *loc.* cit., pp. 86-93.

27. Joseph Fuchs, "The Absoluteness of Moral Terms," *Gregorianum* 52 (1971) 431-441. Fuchs explicitly affirms that Ramsey's analysis of "exceptions" is "the correct one." (p. 441).

28. Bernard Häring, "Dynamism and Continuity in a Personalistic Approach to Natural Law," in *Norm and Context in Christian Ethics*, pp. 199-218, in particular pp. 210-215.

29. Peter Knauer, "The Hermeneutic Function of the Principle of Double Effect," *Natural Law Forum* 12 (1967) 132-162.

30. Grisez, "Toward a Consistent Natural-Law Ethics of Killing," *loc. cit.* in note 22, 64-96. This article expands the reflections offered by the same author in his study on abortion (work cited in note 4.).

31. Here I am summarizing the traditional way of formulating the principle of double effect. Expressed more fully it includes the following elements: (1) The act must not be wrong itself, that is, prescinding from considerations of the evil consequences; (2) the agent's intention must be upright; (3) the evil effect must not be the means to the good effect; and (4) there must be a proportionate reason for doing the act.

32. Daniel Callahan, *Abortion: Law, Choice, and Morality* (New York: Macmillan, 1970), p. 429. A superb critique of Callahan's position so destructive of the sanctity of life is given by Ramsey, "Abortion: A Review Article," *The Thomist* 37 (January, 1973) 174-226, in particular pp. 208-210 on Callahan's understanding of the principle of double effect.

33. William Van der Marck, *Love and Fertility* (New York: Sheed and Ward, 1965), pp. 44-58, for whom the good serving as the proportionate reason is the building up of community. See also his more recent *Toward a Christian Ethic* (New York: Newman, 1967), pp. 41-80.

34. Cornelius Van der Poel, "The Principle of Double Effect," in Charles Curran, editor, *Absolutes in Moral Theology?* (Washington: Corpus, 1968), pp. 186-209. See also his *Search for Human Values* (New York: Newman, 1971), pp. 40-60. Van der Poel's criterion is quite similar to that of Van der Marck, for he places it in the "well-being of the individual and human society," his "norm for moral evaluation" *(Search, p. 56).

35. Bruno Schüller, "Typen ethischer Argumentation in der katholischen Moraltheologie," Theologie und Philosophie 45 (1970) 526-550, and "What Ethical Principles Are Universally Valid?" *Theology Digest* 19 (1971) 23-28.

36. Van der Poel, *Search* . . ., p. 57.

37. The articles on which McCormick comments are "Typen ethischer Argumentation . . ." (cited in note 35) and "Direkte Tötung-indirekte Tötung," *Theologie und Philosophie* 47 (1972).

38. Fuchs, *art. cit.* in note 27.

39. Richard A. McCormick, "Notes on Moral Theology," *Theological Studies* 33 (1972) 68-119.

40. McCormick, *Ambiguity in Moral Choice* (Milwaukee: Marquette University Press, 1973), the 1973 Pere Marquette Lecture in Theology.

41. Fuchs, *art. cit.,* 444.

42. McCormick, "Notes on Moral Theology," *loc. cit.,* 74-75.

43. McCormick, *Ambiguity in Moral Choice,* pp. 14-36, where he criticizes the views of Van der Marck and Van der Poel. McCormick admits the validity of the distinction between what he calls an "intending" and a "permitting" will. The first does directly intend the evil that is caused, whereas the latter does not. He argues (pp. 72, 87 ff) that an intending will bespeaks a greater willingness that the evil occur, a greater endorsement or ratification of the evil. He likewise argues (pp. 62-65) that a greater or more serious proportionate reason is demanded when the will directly intends evil and does not merely permit it, but his fundamental argument is that this proportionate reason or higher good is, when the chips are down, *the* morally decisive element (see, for instance, p. 65 and the other places cited in note 65 below).

44. McCormick, *Ambiguity* . . . pp. 55-65, where he qualifies his earlier (in his *Theological Studies* article) appraisal that Schüller's views were "absolutely correct" and develops his argument that in instances where the evil is directly intended (by an intending will) a stronger or more serious proportionate reason is demanded than in instances when the evil is merely permitted.

45. McCormick, *Ambiguity* . . ., pp. 78-79.

46. Fuchs, *art. cit.*, 444.

47. McCormick, *Ambiguity* . . ., pp. 83-84.

48. Fuchs, *art. cit.*, 445.

49. McCormick, "Notes on Moral Theology," *loc. cit.*, 75.

50. *Ibid.*, 76.

51. *Ibid.* Later, in his *Ambiguity*, McCormick tentatively accepts the criteria for the unity of the act as stipulated by Grisez (see below), but his acceptance of these criteria does not lead him to change his evaluation of the rightness of directly doing evil when this is demanded in order to secure a higher good.

52. McCormick, "Notes on Moral Theology," *loc. cit.*, 71.

53. *Ibid.*, 70-71.

54. Grisez, "Toward a Consistent Natural-Law Ethics of Killing," *loc. cit.*, 76-77.

55. *Summa theologiae*, 2-2, 64, 7, and Grisez's commentary in "Toward a Consistent Natural-Law Ethics of Killing," *loc. cit.*, 73 ff.

56. "Notes on Moral Theology," *loc. cit.*, 74-75.

57. McCormick, *Ambiguity* . . ., pp. 50-53.

58. Grisez, "Toward a Consistent . . .," *loc. cit.*, 88. See also his study on abortion, pp. 333-334.

59. Grisez, "Toward a Consistent . . .," *loc. cit.*, 94-95.

60. Ramsey, in his "Abortion: A Review Article," *loc. cit.*, note 32, objects to one of the tests that Grisez proposes to determine whether an act *is* in fact a unified act in which the evil is only a partial aspect. This test is whether any other human act, one's own or another's, need intervene or could intervene to bring about the good effect. Ramsey believes that this is too stringent a requirement and offers cases that he thinks justifiable but that he believes could not be justified if this requirement is demanded. For Ramsey the "crucial" test "is not . . . whether the death-dealing act may precede the life-saving component of the same human action . . . but whether in (justifiably) doing the deadly deed, the target is upon that life or upon what it is doing to another life" (p. 221 in Ramsey's article). Ramsey, I believe erroneously, concludes in his

article (pp. 224-226) that Grisez's position on abortion, because of Grisez's way of describing the requirements for an act in which the evil is indirectly intended, is paradoxically similar to that of Judith Thompson in her "Defense of Abortion" in *Philosophy and Public Affairs* (Fall, 1971) 47-66. My reason for saying this is that I think Ramsey fails to pay serious enough attention to Grisez's insistence that an abortion properly describable as "indirectly intended" might nevertheless be immoral on other grounds. Even Ramsey's analysis shows that his disagreement with Grisez is not over the requirements for the act's unity. The type of justifiable abortion that Ramsey admits in the cases of a woman with a misplaced appendix or a ruptured aorta is truly describable in Grisez's terms as a unified act having as one aspect an evil consequence (the death of the fetus) and a good consequence as another (the removal of a force periling the life of a mother and rendering impossible the surgical operation to which she is entitled). The difference between Ramsey and Grisez would center more properly on the "proportionate reason" that is also demanded if one is rightfully to do something that inescapably causes evil. But both Grisez and Ramsey demand, in addition to a proportionate reason—which for them is not some kind of "higher good" that functions as an absolute but is rather a situation in which a really basic human good is being seriously jeopardized—the avoidance of directly willing and directly doing the evil as such *(in se)* and the doing of what is, in and of itself, in a sense to be developed below, ordered to the doing of the good.

61. Some of these similarities have been spelled out in the preceding note. A fundamental agreement is that Ramsey and Grisez both demand that the taking of the life of one human being by another or, in general, any doing of the deed that causes evil, must, if it is to be justifiable, be "indirect". Ramsey acknowledges this in his *Thomist* article, p. 220.

62. Ramsey, "The Morality of Abortion," in James Rachels, editor, *Moral Problems* (New York: Harper & Row, 1971), pp. 20-21.

63. *Summa theologiae*, 1-2, 20, 2.

64. This is indicated in their analyses. See in particular McCormick, *Ambiguity in Moral Choice*, pp. 95-96, 98-102.

65. McCormick, *Ambiguity*, pp. 78-79.

66. Even Donald Evans admits this in an article critical of the position taken by Ramsey. See Evans, "Paul Ramsey on Exceptionless Moral Rules," *American Journal of Jurisprudence* 16 (1972) 184-214.

112

Chapter Five:

BECOMING HUMAN IN A REAL WORLD

Toward the end of our discussion of man's moral existence as a conscientious being, attention was called to the words of Paul in Romans: "I do not understand my own actions. For I do not do what I want, but I do the very thing I hate. . . . I can will what is right, but I cannot do it. For I do not do the good I want, but the evil I do not want is what I do" (Romans 7:15-19). Paul's words, I believe, accurately describe a genuine human experience. There are times in our lives when we *know* that we ought to do something or ought not to do something, but we are overcome by a sense of impotency, of powerlessness, and we do things even while we hate ourselves for doing them.

The truth in Paul's words may become clearer if we advance some examples. There are surely many men, for instance, who really love their wives and their families and want to act responsibly toward them. Yet they may be inclined to pursue other women; they may become carried away, as it were, at the sight of a beautiful woman, particularly if they have just had a drink or two and possibly have recently experienced difficulties at home. It is quite conceivable that some men really hate themselves for their propensity in this regard and want to stop —and they are, indeed, to some extent at least, free and responsible in their acts—yet the living context of their moral lives may exert a profound influence on their actions. If they are fortunate enough to have some true friends who will strengthen their resolve and help them stay away from places where they could too easily satisfy their momentary desires, the likelihood of their success in avoiding the chase and of giving themselves to the task of making their family life one of joy and peace is far greater than it is for those who lack such friends and instead are necessarily put in the company of persons who treat the entire matter as a joke.

Or take a girl, a senior in high school, who becomes pregnant. She is not married, does not love the boy who is the father of her child, has legitimate desires for a career. She is placed in a terrible, agonizing position, yet she does not want to take an easy way out of her predicament and have an abortion. If she can count on the love of her family, the help of her friends and relatives, support from persons who respect her as a human being, she is much less likely to have an abortion than is another girl, placed in the same terrible situation, who would be thrown out of her home if her parents discovered that she was pregnant, made the butt of scurrilous jokes, and urged by her closest friends to have an abortion, even if she may not really want to herself.

These examples help show the truth in Paul's words. They likewise support the view of John Macquarrie that we live our lives as moral beings within a living framework wherein we discover both enabling and disabling factors, where we are confronted by the reality of both grace and sin.[1] Before considering in more detail the role of these enabling and disabling elements within our moral environment, however, it will be useful to examine, at least briefly, the question of human freedom. Many influential thinkers, of course, deny that men are free or, indeed, truly responsible for their actions. The famous behaviorist psychologist B. F. Skinner, for example, has recently urged that we go "beyond freedom and dignity," in the sense that these notions are simply illusory and meaningless, in order to construct a society in which environmental factors, scientifically arranged, will necessitate the "right" patterns of behavior in that animal we call man.[2] The underlying rationale of Skinner's proposal is that human behavior, human deeds and acts, are simply the function of heredity and environment and that, given the knowledge of man's biological heritage and a properly ordered environment, "right" behavior will inevitably ensue. This rationale is clearly set forth in an important article by two of Skinner's behaviorist colleagues, Jack Michael and Lee Meyerson, who write:

It is necessary to understand at the outset that the familiar characterization of behavior as a function of the interaction of hereditary and environmental variables is accepted, not with the lip service that is sometimes given before fleeing to hypothetical constructs of inner behavior determiners [free will] that are neither heredity nor environment, but with utmost seriousness.[3]

These writers continue by describing the use of discriminative stimuli in the environment to "shape" or "control" human behavior. Their description of this process clearly shows that for them human freedom is nonexistent, the result of a faulty analysis of the causal factors of human behavior. Although the passage is somewhat technical, it is useful to cite it at some length, for it illuminates quite well the attitude toward human behavior and its causes typical of the behaviorist school and shared by a considerable number of people today. They write:

To produce new behavior . . . or behavior that has not appeared in the response repertoire before, it is sufficient to selectively reinforce one of the variations in the topography which resulted from the previous reinforcement, while allowing the other variations to extinguish. This has the effect of producing a further class of variations from which one may again differentially reinforce some and allow others to extinguish and so on. . . . This procedure for producing new behavior is called *shaping*. It is the technique which animal trainers use to produce unusual and entertaining behaviors in their subjects, and it is the technique whereby humans acquire the complex response topographies of speech, athletic abilities and other motor skills. . . . Although the emphasis in describing operant behavior has been on the reinforcement occurring subsequent to the response, stimulus control is implied in the phrase concluding the principle of operant conditioning—if an operant response is followed by reinforcement it is more likely to occur *under similar conditions in the future*. The simplest principle of stimulus control is that the future probability of response is highest when the stimulus conditions resemble most closely those existing at the moment of previous reinforcement. The expression "resemble most closely" must be analyzed in some detail. . . . By skilled use of the procedures of reinforcement and extinction . . . we can bring about the more precise type of stimulus control that is called *discrimination.* . . . If in the presence of a stimulus a response is reinforced, and in the absence of this stimulus it is extinguished, the stimulus will control the probability of the response in a high degree. Such a stimulus is called a *discriminative stimulus.* Almost all important human behavior is under the control of discriminative shaping, particularly for motor skills; the educator's major efforts are directed toward the development of discriminative repertoires, or in more common terminology, knowledge.[4]

This passage is, as noted already, quite technical. Yet its major thrust is clear. Human behavior is controlled not by the human agent *but by reinforcing stimuli in the environment.* Men do what they do not because they intelligently and freely choose to do this rather than that, but because their deeds are determined to be what they are by factors over which the persons involved have no voice. The deeds men do are not the result of free choices intelligently made but rather the result of environmental conditioners.

B. F. Skinner is by far the most celebrated exponent of this view of human behavior. Consequently it is to our purposes to examine his position in order that we may see more clearly what is at stake. Although not all determinists are Skinnerian behaviorists, all reject human freedom as something illusory, as the heritage of a simplistic view of man, of a naive way of viewing human conduct. With Skinner the determinists repudiate the view that human beings are capable of determining their own lives by making choices that are *theirs*, that incarnate or embody their own personal being and disclose their own identity.[5] But it is important to note that Skinner and other behaviorists, in rejecting human freedom, may be rebelling against a straw man, a figment of their own imaginations and a result of their own misunderstanding of the philosophical tradition that defends human freedom. That this is indeed the case is, I believe, apparent from an examination of Skinner's own writings. Listen, for example, to this instructive passage:

What is being rejected [by those, who unlike Skinner *defend* freedom] is the scientific conception of man and his place in nature. So long as the findings and methods of science are applied to human affairs only in a sort of remedial patchwork, we may continue to hold any view of human nature we like. But as the use of science increases, we are forced to accept the theoretical structure with which science represents its facts. The difficulty is that this structure is clearly at odds with the traditional democratic conception of man. Every discovery of an event which has a part in shaping man's behavior seems to leave so much the less to be credited to the man himself; and as such explanations become more and more comprehensive, the contribution which may be claimed by the individual himself appears to approach zero. Man's vaunted creative powers, his original accomplishments in art, science, and morals, his capacity to choose and our right to hold him responsible for the consequences of his choice—none of these is conspicuous in this new self-portrait. Man, we once believed, was free to express himself in art, music, literature. . . . He could initiate action and make spontaneous and capricious changes of course. Under the most extreme duress some sort of choice remained to him. He could resist any effort to control him, though it might cost him his life. But science insists that action is initiated by forces impinging upon the individual, and that caprice is only another name for behavior for which we have not yet found a cause.[6]

Note that in this passage Skinner equates a free act with "caprice." He also maintains, in other passages,[7] that freedom is "uncaused," that it is behavior that has no assignable causes for its existence. He also stresses the "autonomy" of the free man of tradition, implying that in order to be free men must be totally sufficient for themselves. He is rejecting a view, in other words, that regards men not only as free, in the sense that they are capable of making their own choices and thereby determining their own lives, but as *autonomous*, as agents whose activities are totally uncaused and totally unrelated to factors that exist within the world in which men live. This, I submit, is a misunderstanding of the "literature of freedom," a point to which we shall return shortly.

But Skinner does more than reject the view that man is an autonomous agent. He proposes a view to take its place. On this view, termed scientific by Skinner, "both the responsibility and the achievement" are shifted *from* man *to* "the environment."[8] According to him, "the environment . . . [is] responsible for objectional behavior, and it is the environment, not some attribute of the individual, which must be changed."[9] In his new version of man,

119

the mind simply becomes "an explanatory fiction,"[10] ideas become simply "imagined precursors of behavior,"[11] and intentions exist, not in persons, but in the environmental consequences that reinforce behavior.[12] For Skinner, in short, "it is the environment that acts upon the perceiving person, not the perceiving person who acts upon the environment."[13] In the Skinnerian universe we might with justice say that all power belongs to the environment. As one writer has put it, human beings become Charley McCarthys while the environment becomes the Edgar Bergen who pulls the strings and does the doing.[14]

On the Skinnerian view—and on any deterministic view, it can be said—a person does not refrain from lying or stealing because he has some sense of responsibility and of justice but simply because he fears certain consequences that might happen to him were he to steal or lie. If one does not behave monstrously toward his fellows, it is not because he has any intellectual perception that this is simply inhuman, that it is a mode of acting that does violence to his own being as an intelligent and communicative being, but simply because his fellowmen "have arranged effective social contingencies,"[15] and *why* these contingencies ought to be arranged and not others is a question that Skinner simply cannot answer. Selfless, heroic acts are done by men not because they may love others or because they have chosen to give themselves away to others in love, but simply because the proper set of reinforcing rewards have been operative. This seems to reduce much of what we experience as human beings to the level of mechanics. Any deterministic ethics is, indeed, a "pigeon ethics,"[16] an ethics that not only denies human freedom but effectively denies human agency as well.

Those who defend human freedom do not maintain that man is a totally autonomous being, an agent whose activities are uncaused. Rather they fully accept the fact that factors other than human choice are operative in influencing and, in a sense, determining our acts. One recent defender of human freedom, Juan Luis Segundo, has put things well, I believe, when he says that the problem of human existence is not to be stated in terms of freedom vs. determinism as it is in terms of freedom vs. determinisms. "There is nothing," he writes, "wrong with describing the natural dynamisms, both within and outside me, as determinisms. For the fact is that they are not neutral forces that stand passively at the disposal of some dominating will. But there is a great difference between talking about determinisms and propounding *determinism* (i.e., the nonexistence of liberty). To say that liberty is confronted with determinisms is the same as Paul saying that the inner man is confronted with the law of his members. That does not mean that my liberty is illusory, that it is nothing and cannot be anything. It simply means that it is not a 'faculty' (like memory or senses) which, starting with the use of reason, produces free acts as man gets used to operating reflectively and deliberately rather than on the basis of first impulse."[17] Human freedom, in other words, is not an autonomous liberty, a capricious and uncaused source of agency rooted in some kind of privileged area of the human person. Rather it is rooted in man's existence as a being who can ask questions, who can reflectively grasp himself and the world about him, who can for this reason "transcend" himself and his world and come to possession of himself.

As indicated in the previous paragraph human freedom of choice is rooted in man's existence as an intelligent being. This has been the constant tradition, although understood in differing ways, in a long history of Western philosophy and in the Judeo-Christian view of man. My purpose here is not to demonstrate in any full-scale way that men are free in the sense that they are capable of shaping their own lives by their own choices. Rather I simply want to point to some lines of evidence that support this view of human existence. We can begin by considering the question of instinctive behavior. Here we can observe, with Mortimer Adler, that there is a difference between instinctive mechanisms within the organism that give rise to *patterns of overt behavior* (e.g., the instinct to make nests among birds or to extract honey among bees), and *instinctive or instinctual drives* that are the conative sources of our behavior. The latter include the instinctive drives in men and other animals to preserve the species by sexual activity, to preserve the self by feeding or flight, to ward off enemies by appropriate force, and to associate with members of the same species. These drives are *species predictable,* i.e., they are present in all the members of the same species. In similar fashion true instinctive mechanisms that give rise to patterns of overt behavior are species predictable; i.e., all the members of the same species will *necessarily* act according to these patterns. In man, Adler notes the *only* instances of purely instinctive mechanisms necessarily leading to distinct patterns of overt behavior are such reflex arcs as the pupillary, the salivary, the patellar, and the ciliospinal.[18]

But men are impelled to overt behavior when they are in states of fear, anger, hunger, or sexual arousal, that is, when the instinctive drives common to all the members of the human species are operative. However the precise behavior that different men perform when they are in these states (or that the same man will perform at different times) is *not* species predictable. Rather this behavior consists of voluntary actions that have been learned, are intelligently organized, and may be directed either to the immediate satisfaction of the drive, its postponed fulfillment, or its complete frustration. No animal exerts the mastery over its instinctive drives as does man.

How is this to be explained? Skinner, of course, would explain it *totally* in terms of environmental stimuli, in terms of the reinforcing factors present in the environment. A defender of human freedom will not deny that these environmental factors (and these include other persons and their acts) deeply influence the responses that a person will make and, at times, even necessitate them. But he argues that these factors, while *necessary* factors to be included in any adequate account of human agency, are not the *sufficient* factors to explain the full reality of human deeds. And he points to human intelligence to support his view. Man's power of conceptual thought enables him to devise alternative ways of acting and of dealing with his instinctual urges or drives. It is human intelligence—his existence as the inquiring and questioning animal—that makes freedom possible and, with freedom, the creation of culture and civilization. No other animal, as even Sigmund Freud— himself a determinist—agrees, so suffers the discomforts or pains that result from the domestication and civilization of its instincts. As Freud puts it,

It is impossible to ignore the extent to which
civilization is built upon the renunciation of
instinctual gratifications. . . . It is not easy to
understand how it can become possible for
man to withhold satisfaction from an
instinct. . . .[But] while the intellect is weak in
comparison with instinct, while its voice is

soft as compared to the clamorings of instinct, it does not rest until it has gained a hearing. Ultimately, after several endlessly repeated rebuffs, it succeeds.[19]

It is, I realize, possible to argue with Freud over this interpretation of the reason why man can exercise such mastery over his instinctive drives. Still it must be admitted that the reality he is trying to explain is a phenomenon that we all experience. It suggests that the human intellect exerts a causal influence in human behavior that is incomparable to that of anything in the physical universe. It indicates that man is capable, because of his power of conceptual thought, to think of alternative modes of reacting, of choosing, of behaving. And this is precisely what is at stake in the discussion of human freedom.

Moreover, the indications provided by Freud in his account of man's mastery over his instinctive urges corroborates an older philosophical explanation of man's freedom of choice. According to this explanation, man is a morally free agent because his choices are made among finite goods (even God, as apprehended by human beings in their lives, is apprehended in a finite way, and is *conceptually*, although not *existentially*, a finite good). Because these goods are finite, limited, and hence (at least as intellectually grasped) not *un*limited good, they are also capable of being considered as *less* than the full good that is the goal of man's restless search for fulfillment. They can be regarded as *not* good here and now, so that in making his choices man can consider them as positively evil, even if they really are good. He is not compelled to choose them, because none of them is totally compelling here and now. Man can thus choose evil, knowing it to be evil, but considering it here and now as the good that will bring him the satisfaction that he *wants* right now. And he chooses it because he wills to choose it. The free act is not causeless; it has a cause, the person who chooses, and this person is capable of transcending physical and material limitations precisely because of his being as an intelligent, questioning animal who can raise transcendental questions.[20]

But human freedom is not autonomous. It is confronted by determinisms, as Segundo expresses it. It is a *conditioned* or *situated* freedom or liberty, and this is of enormous significance in our endeavor to understand the meaning of human existence as a moral existence. The situated or conditioned character of our freedom is lucidly set forth by a Dutch theologian, Piet Schoonenberg, in his attempt to think through the meaning of the Christian doctrine of original sin. Schoonenberg seeks to discover how the decision of one person or group of persons can influence or situate or condition the decision of another person yet preserve his basic freedom of choice. He proposes the notion of *situated liberty* as a helpful notion for understanding the dynamics involved:

My free act puts the other in a situation which presents him with good or evil, provides support or withdraws it, communicates values and norms. The situation determines another's freedom insofar as he cannot but respond to the good or evil that confronts him —or else not respond at all. Whatever his decision, it is a matter of choice. *I do not influence his actual reaction, but rather the determinate context in which he freely takes a stand.* The context or situation so links our free decisions that *history itself might be described as the interplay of human decision and situation.*[21]

What does all this mean, and how does it affect our moral lives? Each of us enters a world that is what it is not because of our personal choices and decisions but is what it is, at least in part, because of the personal choices and decisions of others—our parents and grandparents, our forebears, our neighbors. Moreover, we do not choose our parents or our brothers or sisters or early neighbors nor the country in which we are born nor the century. Yet all these factors do influence our decisions, either for good or bad; they provide support or cripple our efforts to do the right thing. It can be suggested, as it has been by writers such as Macquarrie and Schoonenberg, that what we have called disabling and enabling factors are analogs to the theological notions of sin and grace. And these affect us in two principal ways: in our *cognitive* efforts to understand what is right and human and in our *conative* efforts to do what we know to be the human thing to do. We can be helped or crippled in our efforts in both directions.

We live, in short, in a world that has been wounded by sin, by man's failure to respond in trust and love to the words uttered to him by the Father, and uttered to him in the person of his fellowman. Sin is a reality, and its reality has significant repercussions on our struggle to know what we must know if we are to be truly men and to do what we must do if we are to be faithful to our own understanding of ourselves and of our lives. We must note, with Schoonenberg, that the reality of sin and of the sin-filled situation in which we must respond does not destroy our liberty, our freedom. As Schoonenberg puts it, "The situated character of human existence is no contradiction to man's freedom. It is a matter of the determinate conditions that meet man's freedom within its own sphere of action, of that limit upon the objects man encounters and hence the limited number of insights and opportunities they can provide. Men possess a *situated* freedom; every human choice is conditioned by past decisions and restricts future possibilities."[22]

But, as Macquarrie reminds us,[23] the world in which we live is a world in which grace (or the enabling factor or supportive context) is also operative and is, indeed, prior to sin. Who of us has not had the experience of a friend who can help us out, of the encouraging word, the good example, the simple smile? As Christians we know that the God we serve is an Emmanuel, a God *with* us and *for* us, a God who sent us his only Son to become *one* with us. With Paul we can say: "Who will separate us from the love of Christ? . . . I am certain that neither angel nor principalities, neither the present nor the future, nor powers, neither height nor depth nor any other creature will be able to separate us from the love of God that comes to us in Christ Jesus, our Lord" (Romans 8:35-39).

Nonetheless we must take with utmost seriousness the reality of sin and its presence in the world and in the sociopolitical structures of our lives. Here I have in mind not so much our own personal sins, those deeds for which we bear personal responsibility, those evil acts that have been sealed with our own "yes" and ratified in our own consciousness, but what John termed in his Gospel the "sin of the world," the sin that situates our freedom, restricts the possibilities open to us, and at times invites us to evil, even invites us to evil with pressure. Is it possible that the pervasive influence of sin so modifies the objective order that actions, *wrong* in certain aspects and in ideal situations, become *right* for particular individuals?

This is the position that is taken by one of the most

influential and truly outstanding moralists of our day, Charles E. Curran. Curran proposes, within the context of a morality recognizing the pervasive reality of sin, a "theology of compromise." According to this theology of compromise man must do the best he can in a sinful situation. "The destructive and disruptive influence of sin," Curran writes,

frequently prevents man from doing what he would want to do in the given situation. The business man might be forced to make kick-backs in order to stay in business. . . . From one viewpoint the act is good because it is the best that one can do. However, from the other aspect the act is wrong and shows the presence of sin in the given situation. . . . Sin is somehow forcing a person to do what he would prefer not to do under other circumstances. Compromise adopts a middle course between the teaching of the manuals of moral theology and the theory of Professor Fletcher. The moral theology manuals would maintain that such an action is always wrong. Fletcher would maintain that the action is good. Compromise maintains that in a sense the action is good because the person can do nothing else at the present time. However in a certain sense the action is wrong and manifests the presence of sin in the world.[24]

Curran, in stressing the reality of sin, does a great service for moral theology, particularly for those moralists who are working in the Catholic tradition. For too long and for too many, doing the right thing seemed to be somewhat analogous to "pulling oneself up by his own bootstraps." Curran's theology of compromise is intended to pay sufficient attention to the disabling or crippling elements within our lives that affect our acts, to give them the attention they deserve. Nonetheless, his theology of compromise is not, I believe, an adequate or truthful way of facing up to this reality. There are several reasons for this judgment. The first and most important is that it seems to make sin a *right-making* factor in a moral situation. An act that is otherwise wrong (and indeed still remains wrong "from one aspect") *becomes* right because of the presence of sin. The presence of sin, in Curran's view, so alters the objective order that a wrongful act becomes morally justifiable, becomes the right thing to do. This, to me, seems more than paradoxical; it is irreconcilable with an intelligent analysis of the situation.

The matter may be seen more clearly if we look at three expressions: *explain, excuse, justify.* To explain someone's acts is to render them intelligible, to assign reasons for them—whether these acts are right or wrong, human or inhuman. To excuse is to give a reason why someone who does something that really is wrong is not to be held accountable for the wrongness of the deed. He has done something wrongful but has not become, necessarily, wicked or evil in the doing. To justify is to show why an act, ordinarily considered wrong, is right. Curran's theology of compromise is an attempt to justify the deeds that men do because of the presence of sin in the world. It is an attempt to show that these acts are rightful acts, morally good acts. I believe that the presence of sin in the world and in a situation can be an *excusing* factor but not a *justifying* factor. The deed remains wrong if it is indeed an act that an intelligent analysis shows to be wrong by reason of the intent and content of the act, but the one doing it may not fully endorse it, ratify it in his own consciousness, seal it with his own identity. He may be seized by the sense of impotence or powerlessness to which Paul refers in the passage from Romans cited at the beginning of this chapter. But this does not, in my judgment, change the character of the act itself. It remains wrong, because it is a wrongful act, that is, an act wronging others and wronging them (if it is indeed wrong) *directly*.

In addition, in Curran's theology of compromise the person seems robbed *completely* of his liberty; his freedom of action is not only situated but nil, because the "person can do nothing else" at the time. If this is indeed the case, then obviously this affects the moral character of the act, for one of the necessary conditions that *must* exist if an act is to be a moral or human act is that it embodies some degree of human freedom. To the extent that an act is not free it is not a moral act, not an expression of a person's identity as a moral being.

Although I am not able, for these reasons, to accept Curran's theology of compromise, it is a significant attempt to come to grips with a very real problem, or better, mystery. For it points to the living tension, indeed the agony, of our moral lives. What Curran is trying to say, I believe, is that at many times individuals do things that really are wrong; they are wrong because of reality- or truth-making factors; they make one directly attack some basic human good. Nonetheless the persons involved do not really ratify in their heart, in the core of their conscience, in their deep-seated self-awareness, the evil that they are doing. They are not, in and through their acts, making themselves *wicked*. It is surely possible, for instance, for a young girl, alone and frightened, under intense pressure from her family and "friends," to consent to the abortion of her illegitimate child. She may not really want to have an abortion; she may even persuade herself possibly that abortion is not an act that kills human life but is rather to be considered as a form of "postconceptive birth control." This is not, of course, what abortion is, but it is unfortunately possible for a person to convince himself that this is what it is. The situation in an instance of this nature is indeed puzzling, but it is not necessarily an absurdity or self-contradiction. It corresponds, I believe, to experience. Intention, as has been seen previously, relates identical behavior quite differently to our moral being, our moral identity. Although a kickback or the death of a human fetus cannot, in the examples provided, be nonintended in any logical or rational way, inasmuch as an intelligent analysis of the situations discloses that the acts in question are themselves the means to further goals and as means or complete human acts cannot not be intended,[25] human beings do not always act rationally or intelligently. But, and here lies the inadequacy and inaccuracy of Curran's theology of compromise, the activities in question must be judged wrong.

The key issue raised in this entire discussion of the influence of sin and by Curran's theology of compromise is the question of our personal endorsement or ratification of the evil that we do, our willingness to put our own personal seal on the maliciousness or wickedness caused by our deeds. Because we live in a world infected by sin, because we are in many ways morally blinded by sin, enticed by it, pressured by it, we sometimes do things dreadfully wrong but do not accept or even will to accept their wickedness in our hearts.

But it is possible, as we know from experience, for us to fool ourselves. In fooling ourselves we try to ease our conscience by the claim that the evil we do or in which we participate is not really *our* doing but that of someone else. In such instances we really do ratify the evil in our hearts, only we fail to acknowledge this. Because of this human propensity it is important at this juncture to look into another puzzling, exceptionally difficult area of our moral lives in order to see what light we may gain, what truths may be discerned. I have in mind particularly those situations in which evil exists in the world in which we live, an evil to which we do in some sense contribute by participating in the "system," but which is by no means the result of our direct activities. I am thinking of instances in which we are, as it were, "bystanders" to evil, and my purpose is to determine whether there are any guidelines that might be of help to us in wrestling with our own conscience in deciding whether we are "innocent" or "guilty" bystanders.

Numerous examples can be given of this kind of situation. A classic, perhaps, is the situation of the "good" German during the days of the Nazi regime. It must be acknowledged that many Germans did not endorse Hitler's policies of genocide toward the Jews—indeed may have hated these policies—just as many "good" Americans do not endorse racist practices or structures that exploit the weak and the poor. What of the responsibility of the "good" German and the "good" American in such cases? When do we cease being "innocent" bystanders and become "guilty"?

Here the views set forth by John G. Simon, Charles W. Powers, and Jon P. Gunnemann in their perceptive work *The Ethical Investor* seem pertinent. They refer to what they call the "Kew Gardens Principle," a principle so named because of a famous incident illustrating the dilemma confronting us. This occurred several years ago in the Kew Gardens area of New York City when a young woman named Kitty Genovese was attacked and, after a struggle lasting

132

more than a half hour, was killed within eyeshot and earshot of more than thirty people, none of whom wanted to become "involved." According to these authors the Kew Gardens Principle is useful in determining when our failure to respond to a social injury being done by others to another human being becomes morally culpable—when, in short, we ourselves incur responsibility for the evil being done. This principle includes four elements: need, proximity, capability, and last resort.[26] A comment on each will help us understand the meaning of this principle.

It is difficult to give a precise definition of *need*. Nonetheless, as intelligent beings capable of raising questions about our experience and as beings who are called upon to be attentive, reasonable, and responsible, we can tell when our fellow human beings are in need. From previous discussions we have already some notion of the basic human needs that are correlated to basic human goods, goods such as life and health, knowledge, friendship, justice. By being attentive to experience we can tell when these goods are being destroyed in others and when others' legitimate pursuit of these goods is being wrongfully frustrated or effectively denied by others. The person in need is a person crying for help; his cry demands a response.

Proximity, of course, conveys a spatial image, and proximity in space *is* a relevant factor in determining our responsibilities in answering needs. Obviously if we are in a boat with a life preserver and see a person drowning several yards away from us, we are in a situation where a human being is in need and we are proximate to that person. But, as the authors of the Kew Gardens Principle note,

Proximity is largely a function of notice: we hold a person blameworthy if he knows of imperilment and does not do what he reasonably can do to remedy the situation. . . . Notice does not exhaust the meaning of proximity, however. . . . Ignorance cannot always be helped, but we do expect certain persons and perhaps institutions to look harder for information about critical needs.[27]

We can say, then, that proximity is primarily a matter of being consciously aware of the need other people have for help; it is a *noetic* proximity. And being consciously aware of their needs is itself a matter for conscientious reflection. It can be said that this conscious awareness is of two kinds, actual and constructive. There is no necessity to enlarge on actual awareness or notice, for this is immediately evident to anyone in a situation, but constructive awareness needs clarification. A person can be said to be constructively aware of the needs of others if it can be truly said of this person, or group of persons, that he or they *ought* to know of those needs by reason of position in society, background, education, etc. It can be said that the leaders of a society, and perhaps particularly the leaders of the Christian community, are in a state of constructive notice or awareness of the real needs of human beings within that society that are not being met, that are being frustrated by the actions of others.

In connection with the proximity to others' needs that results from a noetic awareness of those needs, some comments on the role of law are in order. It is true that one cannot legislate morality in the sense that it is possible to change people's hearts and attitudes by legislative fiat. But the law can make public that certain human needs exist and that the goods correlative to these needs are the basis of true human rights, rights that are protectable and demand the

134

respect of all the members of a society. The law, in other words, can put people on constructive notice that human rights are entailed in public affairs, in the distribution of the goods of a society, and in the access of all the people of the society to those goods.

Capability, of course, refers to the ability of an individual or group of individuals to help a person or group of persons known to be in need. Here we run into a very serious human problem, namely, the tendency to believe, or succeed in making oneself think that he believes, that nothing that he can do can be of help. There is no easy solution to this difficulty, but it is a matter of conscientious responsibility to recognize this tendency and to counter it by a realistic, that is, truthful appraisal of the situation. "There's nothing that I can do" is too frequently an easy way out of very agonizing situations. Possibly there is nothing that one can do, and no one is obliged to do the impossible: *ought* implies *can*. But human beings are creative, imaginative beings, and one of the most urgent tasks of ethics, in particular Christian ethics, is to devise meaningful alternatives to the crucially important problems of human injustice and participation in the injustices rooted in society.

To determine whether people in need find their "last resort" in us is, of course, another immensely difficult question to determine, and it becomes more difficult the more complex the situation. But, as Gunnemann, Simon, and Powers remark, "Failure to act because one hopes someone also will act—or because one is trying to find out who is the last resort—may frequently lead to a situation in which no one acts at all."[28] There is the tendency to "pass the buck." But at times we must, with Harry Truman, acknowledge that the "buck stops here." A useful clue for determining whether, in fact, we are the last resort, is given by our authors, who write: "This fact

135

[the pass-the-buck mentality that leads nowhere] places more weight on the first three features of the Kew Gardens Principle in determining responsibility, and *it creates a presumption in favor of taking action* when these three conditions are present" (emphasis added).[29]

A final comment on the Kew Gardens Principle is desirable. The Christian community, the gathering of those who are seeking to respond to the good news incarnated in Jesus, has a special responsibility in meeting the needs of human beings who are being wronged by the actions of others, and this responsibility is especially incumbent on the leaders of this community, both clerical and lay. From the very fact that a person is a Christian he is a state of "constructive notice" of the needs of others. One of the tasks of the Christian community is to provide the support, the enabling factors, that men need both to know what they are to do if they are to be fully men and to be able to do what they know they are to do.

It can be said, in fact, that the heroic, agapeically inspired actions of individual men and groups make it possible for others to do what justice requires. Let me explain this by way of an example. In the early 1950's, for example, Jim Crow laws were on the books in the Southland. According to these laws the toilet facilities of public buildings were segregated, and in some public facilities, such as gasoline stations, there were toilet facilities only for white people. It is certainly possible that an individual service station owner could come to the realization that this was an unjust situation, that the refusal to allow certain persons, simply because of their color, to use these facilities, was wrongful, dehumanizing. He may have *wanted* to break from this pattern of behavior, and have even hated himself for refusing to let his black customers use the toilets in his station. But he

136

may have experienced a real incapacity, a genuine impotency, to do anything constructive about the matter, simply because he realized that if he did, his station might be destroyed by a Molotov cocktail, his home burned, his wife raped, his children abused. In a sense he simply *could not* do anything about the situation. He lacked the capacity to act, to do what in justice he realized he ought to have done. But because some men were rendered capable of acting heroically, of acting agapeically ("my grace is sufficient for you"), even at the cost of serious threat to their own legitimate pursuits, possibly even at the risk of long prison sentences and even death, the situation was changed so that *others* could be required in justice to do what was right, what was human. In other words, Christian love or agape can be an enabling factor, it can bring about changes in the sociopolitical structures of a society so that the realm of justice can be enlarged. This realm is enlarged when the structures of a society enable persons to do what they know to be the right or human thing to do.

The foregoing reflections on the character of our moral lives and the meaning of our existence as moral beings by no means offer an adequate account of what our moral existence entails. Yet they do, I hope, offer us some insight into the character of our existence as moral beings. The vocation of every human being is to close the gap between the empirical and the normative human, to become the kind of being that a human being is meant to be. The Christian knows in a more explicit and formal way what man is meant to be than does the non-Christian, because the incarnation of God's Word, his othering of himself in what is not himself, namely man, illumines the meaning of human existence. But we also know that in order for us to become the kind of beings we are meant to be we need help, we need a supportive context. We need what theologians call grace. And we also know that in our struggle to become more human, we are crippled by the actions of others as well as by our own actions, by what theologians call sin. But for the Christian (and for all men) there is hope, the element that Macquarrie calls the "dynamic" of our moral lives.[30] Hope is not an easy optimism, an ostrich-like attitude that tries to brush aside sin and evil, the suffering of the innocent, and the terrible agonizing dilemmas that confront human beings. Rather it is the conviction that the struggle of men to free themselves from the determinisms that frustrate their endeavors to know who they are and to do what they are to do *can* succeed because their struggle is not theirs alone. The God of Christian faith, the one true God of all men, is a God who is with and for men; he is our Emmanuel, offering us his life and offering it to us *now*. It is for this reason that a hallmark of a Christian ethics, of a truly human ethics, is its *eucharistic* character, its spirit of thanksgiving and joy.

Notes

1. See John Macquarrie, *Three Issues in Ethics* (New York: Harper & Row, 1970), pp. 119-125.

2. See B. F. Skinner, *Beyond Freedom and Dignity* (New York: Knopf, 1971).

3. Jack Michaels and Lee Meyerson, "A Behavioral Approach to Human Control," in Roger Ulrich, Thomas Stachnik, and John Mabry (eds.), *Control of Human Behavior* (Glenview, Ill.: Scott, Foresman, and Co., 1966), p. 23.

4. *Ibid.*, pp. 26-27.

5. At this point it may be useful to offer some clarifying comments concerning the meaning of freedom. A very helpful source on this topic is the two-volume work by Mortimer Adler, *The Idea of Freedom* (New York: Doubleday, 1960-1961). According to Adler there are five principal notions of freedom in the history of Western thought. These are: (1) Circumstantial Freedom of Self-Realization. This is a "freedom which is possessed by any individual who, under favorable circumstances, is able to act as he wishes for his own good as he sees it" (II, 5). (2) Acquired Freedom of Self-Perfection. This is "a freedom which is possessed only by those men who, through acquired virtue or wisdom, are able to will or live as they ought in conformity to the moral law or an ideal befitting human nature" (II, 6). (3) Natural Freedom of Self-Determination. This is "a freedom which is possessed by all men, in virtue of a power inherent in human nature, whereby a man is able to change his own character creatively by deciding for himself what he shall do or shall become" (II, 6-7). (4) Political Freedom. This is a "freedom which is possessed only by citizens who, through the right of suffrage and the right of juridical appeal against the abuses of government, are able to participate in making the positive laws under which they live and to alter the political institutions of their society" (II, 8). (5) Collective Freedom. This is a "freedom which will be possessed by humanity . . . in the future, when through the social use of the knowledge of both natural and social necessities, men achieve the ideal mode of association that is the goal of mankind's development and are able to direct their communal life in accordance with such necessities." Of these, the central freedom in our consideration of man's moral life is the natural freedom of self-determination. On this topic, see the recent book by Germain Grisez and Russell Shaw, *Beyond the New Morality: The Responsibilities of Freedom* (Notre Dame, Ind.: University of Notre Dame Press, 1974), Chapter One.

6. B. F. Skinner, "Freedom and the Control of Man," in Ulrich, Stachnik, and Mabry, *op. cit.*, p. 13.

7. Skinner, *Beyond Freedom and Dignity*, p. 19.

8. *Ibid.*, p. 25.

9. *Ibid.*, p. 74.

10. *Ibid.*, p. 24.

11. *Ibid.*, p. 24.

12. *Ibid.*, p. 184.

13. *Ibid.*, p. 188.

14. Daniel C. Maguire, "Pigeon Ethics: The Moral Philosophy of B. F. Skinner," in *The Living Light* 9. 2 (Summer, 1972) 26-32.

15. Skinner, *Beyond Freedom and Dignity,* p. 185.

16. See Maguire, *art. cit.*

17. Juan Luis Segundo, *Grace and the Human Condition* (Maryknoll, N. Y.: Orbis Books, 1973), p. 32.

18. Mortimer Adler, *The Difference of Man and the Difference It Makes* (New York: Meridian, 1968), pp. 274-275.

19. Sigmund Freud, *Civilization and Its Discontents* (New York: Sloan, 1932), p. 137.

20. On this subject see, for instance, Thomas Aquinas, *Summa Theologiae* I, 86, 1-4.

21. Piet Schoonenberg, *Man and Sin* (South Bend, Ind.: University of Notre Dame Press, 1965), p. 105.

22. *Ibid.*, pp. 105-106.

23. Macquarrie, *op. cit.*, pp. 122-125.

24. Charles Curran, "Dialogue with Joseph Fletcher," in his *A New Look at Christian Morality* (South Bend: Fides, 1968), pp. 171-172. See also his "Dialogue with the Homiphile Movement," in *Catholic Moral Theology in Dialogue* (South Bend: Fides, 1972), pp. 215-18.

25. On this, see the discussion of human acts above.

26. John G. Simon, Charles W. Powers, and Jon P. Gunnemann, *The Ethical Investor* (New Haven: Yale University Press, 1972), p. 22.

27. *Ibid.*, p. 23.

28. *Ibid.*, pp. 24-25.

29. *Ibid.*, p. 25.

30. Macquarrie, *op. cit.*, pp. 131-146.

Bibliography

The literature pertinent to the themes discussed here is enormous. The following list represents works that are particularly worth reading.

Introductory works (on the nature of ethical inquiry, the meaning of Christian ethics and its relationship to man's strivings; not all of the works listed are by Christians, but it is crucially important to understand what they have to say and to relate their thoughts to the work of theologians; the titles in this section are particularly pertinent for developing the ideas set forth in Chapter One):

Adler, Mortimer. *The Difference of Man and the Difference It Makes.* New York: Meridian, 1968.

_____ *The Time of Our Lives: The Ethics of Common Sense.* New York: Holt, Rinehart and Winston, 1970; in particular Part Two.

Curran, Charles. *Catholic Moral Theology in Dialog.* South Bend: Fides, 1972; in particular the chapters on humanism, science, and social ethics.

Grisez, Germain and Russell Shaw. *Beyond the New Morality: The Responsibilities of Freedom.* Notre Dame, Indiana: University of Notre Dame Press, 1974.

Gutierrez, Gustavo. *Theology of Liberation*. Mary-knoll, N.Y.: Orbis Books, 1973. Parts 1, 2, and 4 are of importance for the themes of Chapter One.

Macquarrie, John. *Three Issues in Ethics*. New York: Harper & Row, 1970. A beautiful, profound work really indispensable.

McCabe, Herbert. *What Is Ethics All About?* Washington: Corpus, 1969. This superbly written work of profound significance and immensely important.

Murray, John Courtney. *We Hold these Truths*. New York: Sheed & Ward, 1960.

Maritain, Jacques. *The Person and the Common Good*. New York: Scribner's, 1947. A short but rich work, especially valuable for understanding the meaning of man's existence as a being of moral worth.

Rahner, Karl. His articles on "Incarnation" and "Jesus Christ" in volume 3 of *Sacramentum Mundi* (New York: Herder & Herder, 1968) are exceptionally pertinent to the understanding of Chapter One. For a brief introduction to his thought see the chapter devoted to Rahner in my *Christ in Contemporary Thought*. Dayton: Pflaum, 1970.

Segundo, Jaun Luis. *Grace and the Human Condition*. Maryknoll, N.Y.: Orbis Books, 1973.

The Development of Moral Knowledge and the Role of Conscience (Chapters Two and Three)

Much material in the works cited above, particularly in Macquarrie (in particular the chapter on conscience, sin, and grace), McCabe, and Adler, is pertinent to these themes. In addition the following are immensely significant.

Berger, Peter and Thomas Luckmann. *The Social Construction of Reality*. New York: Doubleday, 1965.

D'Arcy, Eric. *Conscience and Its Right to Freedom*. New York: Sheed and Ward, 1965.

Grisez, Germain. *Contraception and the Natural Law*. Milwaukee: Bruce, 1964, in particular Chapter Three, "Three Theories of Natural Law."
_____. *Abortion: The Myths, the Realities, and the Arguments*. New York: Corpus, 1970.

Kohlberg, Lawrence. "Stages of Moral Development as a Basis for Moral Education," in C. M. Beck, B. S. Crittenden, and E. V. Sullivan, eds. *Moral Education: Interdisciplinary Approaches*. New York: Newman, 1972, pp. 23-92.

Lonergan, Bernard. *Method in Theology*. New York: Herder & Herder, 1972.

Nelson, C. Ellis, ed. *Conscience: Theological and Psychological Perspectives*. New York: Newman, 1973. An excellent anthology. He reprints Macquarrie's chapter on conscience from *Three Issues* and includes superb articles by John Glaser, Gregory Zilbourg, Dorothea McCarthy, and many others.

Ethical Methodology (Chapter Four)

Again, many of the writings listed above are very important with respect to this question, in particular the works of Grisez, McCabe, and Lonergan. But the following are absolutely indispensable.

Fletcher, Joseph. *Situation Ethics*. Philadelphia: Westminster, 1965. See also the work he did in conjunction with Thomas Wassmer and edited by William E. May, *Hello, Lovers! An Invitation to Situation Ethics*. New York: Corpus, 1970. As readers will recognize, I believe that this approach is absolutely erroneous, but it is very worthwhile to read its most persuasive presentation.

Fuchs, Josef. "The Absoluteness of Moral Terms," in *Gregorianum* 52 (1971).

D'Arcy, Eric. *Human Acts: An Essay on Their Evaluation*. Oxford: Oxford University Press, 1963. A brilliant, lucid work.

Grisez, Germain. In addition to his works cited above, see also his supremely important article, "Toward a Consistent Natural-Law Ethics of Killing," in *American Journal of Jurisprudence* 15 (1970) 64-96.

McCormick, Richard. *Ambiguity in Moral Choice*. Milwaukee: Marquette University Press, 1973, the 1973 Pere Marquette Lecture in Theology. This expands the views that McCormick has been setting forth in his superb "Notes on Moral Theology" in *Theological Studies* over the past several years.

Ramsey, Paul. "The Case of the Curious Exception," in *Norm and Context in Christian Ethics*, edited by Gene Outka and Paul Ramsey. New York: Scribner's, 1968. A supremely important essay.

_____. *Deeds and Rules in Christian Ethics*. New York: Scribner's, 1967. A masterful work.

_____. "Abortion: A Review Article," in *The Thomist* 37 (January, 1973) 174-226. (In my judgment Grisez and Ramsey are the very best living analysts of moral action writing in English.)

Many of the writings cited previously, in particular those of Curran, McCabe, Macquarrie, Segundo, and Ramsey are very valuable on this question. In addition, the following are particularly significant.

Gunnemann, Jon, Charles Powers, and John Simon. *The Ethical Investor.* New Haven, Conn.: Yale University Press, 1971.

Niebuhr, Reinhold. *Moral Man in Immoral Society.* New York: Scribner's, 1960.

Schoonenberg, Piet. *Man and Sin.* Notre Dame, Ind.: University of Notre Dame Press, 1965.

Ramsey, Paul. *The Just War.* New York: Scribner's. 1968.